Strategic

Effective Deliverance Prayer Tactics - Warfare and Confrontations

Approach to Effective Communication in Prayer

**By:
Dr. Pauline Walley**

Copyright © 2007 by Pauline Walley

Strategic Prayer Tactics II:
Effective Deliverance Prayer Tactics -
Warfare and Confrontations
by Pauline Walley

Printed in the United States of America

ISBN 978-1-60266-026-7
IBSN 1-60266-026-3

All rights reserved solely by the author. The author guarantees all contents are original and do not infringe upon the legal rights of any other person or work. No portion of this book may be reproduced, stored in a retrieval system, or transmitted in any form or by any other means—electronic, mechanical, photocopy, recording or any other—except for brief quotations in printed reviews—without the prior permission of the author. The views expressed in this book are not necessarily those of the publisher.

Unless otherwise indicated, Scripture references are from the New King James version of the Holy Bible. Copyright © 1990, 1985, 1983 by Thomas Nelson, Inc.

www.xulonpress.com

Contents

Acknowledgment ix
Introduction xi

Chapter One: Warfare and Confrontations 17
      Physical Body Equipment 18
      Weapons of Warfare 21
      Choice of Prayer Tactics 23

**Chapter Two: The Purpose of Warfare
    Prayer 37**
      Setting Your Goals...................................37
      Preparing Your Agenda 38

Chapter Three: The War of Eviction 41

Chapter Four: Specific Prayer............................45

Chapter Five: Standing on Scriptures 51

Chapter Six: Speaking with Knowledge and Authority..57

Chapter Seven: War of Words...............................63

Chapter Eight: Difficulties and Interferences..73

Chapter Nine: Legal Grounds...............................77
    Identity Card..78
    Illegal Possessions......................................78
    Indulgence and Diabolism.........................78
    Illegal Open Doors.....................................79

Chapter Ten: Names...83
    Remembering the Dead...............................84
    Haunted Names...84
    Inheritance for Transference......................84
    Transference of Spirit by Name.................85
    Biblical Names..86

Chapter Eleven: Residence and Address............91

Chapter Twelve: Date and Place of Birth..........95

Chapter Thirteen: Spiritual Birth.......................99

Chapter Fourteen: Religious Affiliation...........105

Chapter Fifteen: Marital Status........................109

Chapter Sixteen: Children and Siblings...........113

Chapter Seventeen: Country of Origin............117

Chapter Eighteen: Religious Belief and Idolatry............121

Chapter Nineteen: Family Background............127

Chapter Twenty: Character Inheritance............131

Chapter Twenty-one: Emotional Inheritance............137

Chapter Twenty-two: Material and Financial Inheritance............141

Chapter Twenty-three: Burdens and Concerns............145

Chapter Twenty-four: The Deliverance War............151

Chapter Twenty-five: Prisoners of War............155

Chapter Twenty-six: Deliverance Prayer............161

Chapter Twenty-seven: Prayer of Confrontation............169

Chapter Twenty-eight: Warring with Worship............173

Chapter Twenty-nine: Confronting with Scripture............177

Chapter Thirty: On the Battlefield...................181

Chapter Thirty-one: The Joshua Strategy.......185

Chapter Thirty-two: Jehovah's Strategy.........189

Chapter Thirty-three: Divine Deliverance.......193

Chapter Thirty-four: The Victory....................197

Chapter Thirty-five: Praying with John I........203

Chapter Thirty-six: Praying with Psalm 91 207

Acknowledgments

Special thanks to the Almighty God, who has put in me the spirit of humility to receive teaching and counsel through the power of the Holy Spirit.

Thanks to my parents Bishop Enoch and Felicia Walley and other members of my family for bringing me up in the fear of God.

I hereby express my profound appreciation to the individuals who have stood with me at Overcomers' House and have encouraged me through my valleys and mountains with Pauline Walley Evangelistic Ministries.

These include our partners, supporters, organizers, coordinators and all who are affiliated to Pauline Walley Ministries known as Overcomers around the world.

Special thanks to our coordinators in Europe, Africa, Caribbean, Asia and America for coming on board to support this unique work around the world. I wish I could include all the names of my special lovers, supporters, and international coordinators, but time and space will not permit me to do so. However, I give thanks to all those who have contributed to the progressiveness of my life and ministry.

Special thanks to my *Unique Editor*, Kay Coulter, whose work and advice have been very inspiring and encouraging to me. My appreciation also goes to Rev. John Smith of Diplomat Center, Guyana and Rev. Jim Wong of Singapore for validating my work and ministry.

Introduction

In the early summer of 2003, I had a nudge to stay quiet in the presence of the Lord. As soon as I sat in His presence in my bedroom, He began to speak to me concerning the need to start the School of Strategic Prayer. Immediately, the Lord began to dictate the contents and the details of what I have to be teaching. As He was speaking, I was typing the message on my laptop computer. For three days I was indoors receiving and writing in the presence of the Lord.

Within two weeks I had written about 200 pages of manuscripts that would form the Volumes I and II of the School of Strategic Prayer teaching notes and textbooks. Volume I comprises the Types of Prayer and Tactical Approach, while Volume II is on Warfares and Confrontations, and Volume III is on Intercessions and Supplications.

Everywhere I go, I notice that the attitude of people towards prayer is not very encouraging. Unless people have challenges, they do not see the need to pray. People prefer to pay money to psychics and the clairvoyants to perform spiritual rituals rather than participate in church prayer and give generous offerings.

During my PhD research, I interviewed both unbelievers and churchgoers on issues regarding involvement in church prayer and consulting clairvoyants for help. The result of my interactive research shows that many churchgoers do not know the difference between praying in church and consulting spiritualists/mediums/psychics and spiritual-readers for help.

Some churchgoers confessed that they have always thought that the spiritualists and clairvoyants perform the same function as the church pastor and priest. They refer to the spiritualist as a prophet because the clairvoyant does not only pray but also gives spiritual direction.

People who are used to a quick fix think it is a waste of time to spend much time in prayer. They would rather pay for a prayer service than devote their time to pray.

However, prayer is not only meant to solve problems, prayer is the contact point to get connected to the Almighty God. Prayer is communication between man and God. Prayer brings one into a unique relationship that money cannot buy. Prayer is a forum for a father child relationship. Prayer is an aromatic expression that produces sweet smelling incense.

Beloved, you need to get involved in prayer now. Do not wait until you have problem to show up in the church as though you have a police case. Do not turn the presence of God into a courthouse where you see the priest or pastor as a presiding judge.

Beloved, turn your home into a prayer house instead of a boxing or wrestling ring with witches and demons. Turn your home into a praise worship center instead of an arena of sorrow and pain.

Beloved, it is time for us to understand the meaning of prayer and also to know how to open our mouths for prayer and know what to say in order to overcome our enemy—Satan and his cohorts. There is a time for silent prayer and there is a time for aggressive prayer. We need to know and understand the application of different types of prayer so that we can enjoy our salvation. Many people claim to be Christians, but very few have actually enjoyed the blessings of Christianity. When we strike a difference between the Christian and the churchgoer, we would be able to understand why everyone has not actually been able to taste the joy of salvation.

This book, *Approach to Effective Communication in Prayer*, will teach you how to go into warfare and confront the enemy. It will teach you how to be equipped with the language of war and pull down satanic strongholds.

There are spiritual protocols that we need to observe in order to get things done with our prayers. If we ignore certain spiritual protocols, we break our own legal grounds, which gives the enemy an open door to attack and plunder us. This book is written as a direction from the Most High God in order to help the people who seek deliverance from evil (Matthew 6:13). Therefore, do not despise the instructions given if you really want to obtain results and enjoy your relationship with the Lord.

In the initial chapters of Part I, sample prayers are presented at the end of each discussion to help you to modify your system of prayer, especially if you have difficulty with what to say and how to pray. In the subsequent chapters of Part II, tactical and confrontational prayers are presented in the same manner and for the same purpose.

Also, there is a portion to help you monitor the reactions that take place when you are praying—your feelings, perceptions and pace of the prayer itself. Find out if you did have some form of experiences such as being hilarious, hysterical or excited. Did your body tremble and did you feel lighter than usual? Did you have any form of revelation or hear a voice? Please note your experiences, and analyze everything at the end of each discussion.

Stay blessed and experience a unique encounter with Jesus Christ our Lord and Redeemer as you make use of prayer tactics. Amen!

Prayer Tactics

(Remember to observe the Spiritual Protocol in Chapter One)

State the Problem:
You need to develop your prayer life.

Prayer Focus:
Pray that the Lord will enable you to understand the essence of this book.

- That this book would help you to discover new prayer tactics to confront the enemies of your life.

The Authority of Scripture:
"**Study to show thyself approved unto God . . .**" (2 Timothy 2:15 KJV).

The Prayer:
O Lord and my God, thank you for sustaining my life.

Thank you for giving me this book.

Teach me to understand the purpose of this book.

For the Scripture encourages us to study to show ourselves approved unto God. Therefore, help me to acquire knowledge as I read this book.

And help me to improve my prayer lifestyle.

Also teach me new prayer tactics that I may be able to confront the devil and take back whatever he has stolen from me.

In Jesus' name I pray. Amen!

Observations – write your experience after the prayer:

_____
_____
_____

Achievements – what did you gain from this prayer?

_____
_____
_____

The Results

_____
_____
_____

CHAPTER ONE

Warfare and Confrontations

—⚡—

Warfare and confrontation are the activities of armed forces and military aggression in the spiritual realms. The act of deliverance ministration is a battlefield that involves Godly strongmen against satanic strongmen and their strongholds. (See my book, *Pulling Down Satanic Strongholds*, for details on Stronghold and Strongmen).

Warfare and confrontations are a war of words that demands that you speak to the enemy in legal languages that are biblical. Confrontation means you are commanding and instructing the enemy with defiance. This is where you need to open your mouth and make declarations that causes every knee to bow and tremble at the mention of the name of Jesus Christ.

The giant, Goliath the Philistine, engaged the Israelites in a confrontation, to which David responded before they went into physical combat where they had to use ammunitions. While the United States is at war with Bin Laden and the al-Qaeda, Bin Laden, who is said to be in hiding, has been confronting United States with a war of words. Recently, the leader of Hesbollah (a supposed terrorist organization) has been confronting both Israel and United States with a war of words.

Warfare is not fought physically as in a boxing or a wrestling ring but with Scriptural language that demands physical involvement: such as reading and studying with prayer and fasting. Warring in prayer demands body movement and speaking the Word of God from the Scriptural perspective.

Physical Body as Equipment

Although spiritual battles are not fought with the physical mind and flesh, yet the prayer of warfare and confrontations demand the involvement of a person's physical body as in military actions and tactics: such as walking and marching around; pacing up and down; running, jumping and galloping; and also throwing hands around as in boxing and wrestling. The prayer of warfare and confrontations involve military aggressiveness that demands the use of the hands and feet. Joshua and King David were biblical warriors who displayed military aggression against the enemies of Israel.

Besides military aggressiveness that involves the hands and feet, other physical weapons that are needed for warfare and confrontation include your mouth, your tongue, your voice, your utterance and your language.

Your Mouth: In order to confront the enemy in a war, you need to open your mouth and speak out.

When you open your mouth, you are opening fire on the enemy. The action of opening your mouth is like a soldier pointing his gun to shoot at an enemy. **Isaiah 9:12 states, "And they shall devour Israel with an open mouth . . . ."**

Your Tongue: Your tongue is the burner that ignites the fire that comes out of your mouth. Speaking in diversity of tongues carries different wave lengths in the spiritual realm. There is a time to speak with the understanding and a time to speak in tongues. Speaking in diversity of tongues is like releasing missiles and grenades into the camp of the enemy. When you open your mouth to speak with diversity of tongues, the Lord will fill it with fiery words and that throw your enemy into confusion. **Psalm 81:10 declares, "Open your mouth wide, and I will fill it.**

Your Voice: When you open your mouth in a war of confrontation against the enemy, the Lord will use your voice; and your voice will sound like a roaring lion, and the noise of it shall cause disaster in the midst of your enemies (**Jeremiah 25:30-32**). The lion is known as the king of the animals because the sound of its voice causes all animals to tremble and run for their lives.

Your Utterances: During warfare and confrontations, the Lord will speak through you; and your utterance would cause the enemy to tremble. The language of war is not words of passion but rather words of power that have the ability to break the chains of captivity and pull down satanic strong' (**Joel 3:16**). The purity of your heart and utter are weapons against the enemy.

When you open your mouth during warfare and confrontation:

The purity of your words defeats the enemy. **Job 33:2-3** states,

> **Now, I open my mouth;**
> **My tongue speaks in my mouth.**
> **My words come from my upright heart;**
> **My lips utter pure knowledge.**

Open your mouth and enter into warfare with praise worship as indicated in **Psalm 51:15**:

> **O Lord, open my lips,**
> **And my mouth shall show forth Your praise.**

Open your mouth and make declarations to set the captive free as in **Psalm 78:2**,

> **I will open my mouth in parable;**
> **I will utter dark sayings of old.**

Also **Proverbs 31:9** states,

> **Open your mouth, judge righteously,**
> **And plead the cause of the poor and needy.**

If you want God to use your mouth in battle, then you must learn to open your mouth. The Lord commanded the prophets of old to open their mouths and speak to situations. **Ezekiel 3:27** states **"But**

when I speak with you, I will open your mouth, and you shall say to them . . . ."

Weapons of Warfare

The governments of nations and the secular world equip their armed forces by training them to combat the enemy on battlegrounds. Whether there is rumor of war or not, the governments of nations equip their guards against emergency. Besides equipping, armed forces are also given instruments of weaponry to war against the enemy.

Similarly, the spiritual realms have equipment and weapons for warring and confronting the enemy. The weapons of our warfare are not carnal but spiritual. The spiritual weapons used by Christian soldiers include: the Word of God, the Name of Jesus, the Blood of Jesus, Oil, Spiritual Gifts and Revelations (See details in my books: *When Satan Went to Church* and *Solutions: Deliverance Ministration to Self and Others*).

The Word: Jesus Christ is the Word of God and the Bread of Life. Knowledge is power; therefore a Christian soldier must be acquainted with the Word of God in order to be able to confront the enemy and war against satanic cohorts.

The Name: The Name of Jesus Christ is power and authority. There is no other name above the name of Jesus. The name of Jesus is a weapon against the enemy. Worship, honor and reverence the Name of Jesus if you want to experience the power of deliverance.

The Blood: Like the name of Jesus Christ, the blood of Jesus Christ is power and authority. The blood of Jesus Christ is healing and deliverance. By faith we drink ordinary wine produced by some individuals as a symbol of the blood of Jesus. Similarly, you can drink the blood of Jesus by faith as you worship the blood of Jesus and reverence the power in the blood through the death of Jesus Christ on the cross of Calvary.

The Oil: The smell of olive oil repels demons if the blood of Jesus is pleaded upon it to symbolize the presence and power in the name of Jesus Christ.

Spiritual Gifts and Revelations: Spiritual gifts and revelations are very crucial weapons for warring and confronting the enemy. Without the spiritual gifts, one cannot hear instructions from God and follow the direction of the combat to conquer the enemy. Revelations will enable you to understand the wiles of the enemy as to how to mount up strategies against powers and principalities of darkness.

Time of Warfare

There are different types of wars that are fought at certain periods and hours of the day and night. It is very import that anyone going into warfare must discern the strategies of the times and seasons that certain wars should be fought in order to overcome the enemy. When the children of Israel were journeying through the wilderness to the Promise Land, the Lord gave the pillar of fire for protection at night and the pillar of cloud for protection in the day (**Exodus 13:22**). Also, **Psalms 91** reveals that there is a war that takes place in the midnight hour and a battle that is fought in the day time.

Midnight War (12:00 midnight to 5:00 a.m.): If Psalm 91 declares that there is a terror that takes place at night; it means we need to discern through spiritual gifts and revelations what happens when human beings are sleeping. Jesus went into the garden to pray through the night because there was a war to be fought at the midnight hour. While Jesus was praying, the disciples were sleeping because they did not understand the importance of midnight prayer (**Luke 6:12-15**).

Scripture reveals that anytime the children of Israel planted their crops, the Midianites went into their farmland at night to destroy their produce. The destruction that came upon the Israelites at night caused them to be impoverished. The spirit of poverty attacks individuals and businesses at midnight. Thieves usually burgle at night when everybody is sleeping (**1 Thessalonians 5:2**). The night represents darkness. The spirit of darkness is a spirit of robbery. Witches and wizards often operate at the midnight hour. Gideon received a command to deliver the Children of Israel from the Midianites and the Amalekites; he used the night strategy to establish himself among his people and also to conquer the enemy of Israel (**Judges 6 and 7**). To stop the operation of a witchcraft spirit around your home, you must **launch out against the enemy between the hours of 12:00 midnight and 6:00 a.m**.

Mid-day War (12:00 noon to 2:30 p.m.): Psalm 91 also states that there are wars that take place during the day: "**The arrow that flies by day.**" The Philistine giant confronted Israel with a war of words, and David responded to his confrontation by day and defeated him. The hours of warring during the day time are between 12.00 noon and 2.30 p.m. There are people who cannot stay by themselves by day or by night, because they often suffer evil interferences or see demonic apparitions.

War of the Business Realm: Usually there is a combined war of night and day, whereby certain wars are fought in the spirit realm by night; and the physical manifestation takes place during the day. For instance, wars of the business realms take place in the night, and the results are manifested in the marketplace during the day. When wars are fought are night, some people will perceive the impact in their dreams. God allows his children to see the wars so that we can rise up and counter the wars and stop the manifestations. The essence of revelation is to redeem the consequences and change evil situations around.

War of the Graveyard: Also the workers of iniquity and satanic cohorts usually operate at graveyards in the middle of the night. Incantations of death and disasters are made against people at night. Wickedness is carried out at night. Satanic strongmen operate in darkness. On many occasions, people usually have dreams in which they see themselves in coffins or buried in graveyards before disasters that could lead to their deaths happen in the physical realm. The graveyard or monument represents the spirit of death and disaster.

These categories of evil entities operate at night and manifest during the day. Both midnight and midday warfare and confrontations are needed to quell the manifestation of the war of the graveyard in our homes.

The Battlefield

There are battles that should be fought in your home, and there are wars to be fought in prayer houses and in church auditoriums. You need to be careful of the type of battle that you take into your home, especially when you have teenagers or delinquent individuals around your home.

Your Home is supposed to be a resting place. Do not turn your home into a battleground if you have unbelievers in your home. You need to discern the kinds of war around you, and fight each battle at the appropriate time so that members of your household will not be drawn into unnecessary battles. There are wars that require the involvement of everyone in your home, and there are battles that should not be initiated around your home, otherwise innocent persons will be captured as prisoners of war.

The Church Auditorium is the house of the Lord and has the fire of both the ministers and intercessors burning on the altar of incense. Scripture declares that one shall chase a thousand and two shall chase ten thousand (Deuteronomy 32:30). The corporate prayers of all the church brethren goes against the enemy like fiery brimstone.

The Prayer Room is a place dedicated for prayer activities in the homes, in institution buildings and on church premises. Since a place has been dedicated to prayer, there is supposed to be enough fire to carry on different levels of warfare and confrontations. However, the blood of Jesus must be pleaded constantly to keep the pure fire burning on the altar of incense unto the Lord.

Summary from Volume I

This book is a continuation of Volume I in the School of Strategic Prayer series. Therefore, you need to read Volume I in order to understand the pattern set out in Volume II. Below is a brief summary of the requirements discussed in Volume I that will boost your approach to effective prayer.

Approach to Prayer and Spiritual Protocol
(Excerpt from Volume I)

Stating the Problem
The need you take into prayer must be stated. That need is a problem that needs to be solved. In order for your need to be met, you must state the problem in plain words with clarity and brevity.

Prayer Focus
Having stated the problem or the need to be met, the next thing to do is to break down the need into units in order for you stay focused. Breaking down your prayer need into points or smaller units helps you to put together the details of your need and also to pray with specific words with understanding of

what you actually desire and what you want God to do for you.

Authority of Scripture

For effectiveness, it is very important to pray with Scripture. Praying with Scripture enables us to declare our spiritual authority in Christ Jesus. It enables us to remind God about His Word and what He has spoken concerning us.

The Prayer

Now that you have set out your goal by identifying your need and drawing up your focus, you can decide to pray with your understanding and also in tongues so that the Holy Spirit can help you out. In prayer, we are either presenting our requests, making petitions on behalf of others or warring and confronting the enemy. The way we communicate with God is very important.

The Process of Cleansing

It is important to observe the process of sanctification and purification any time we set out for prayer. Cleansing is necessary because God is holy, and we must approach His presence with cleanness of character and purity of our hearts (Leviticus 19:2). God will not use unclean vessels, just like humans will not eat or drink from unclean utensils. Therefore, self-cleansing is very crucial if we must enjoy the presence of the Lord during prayer (Leviticus 16:30). The process of cleansing includes:

Confession of sin: to admit a fault by presenting our guilt before the Lord. We state exactly what we have done wrong in order to receive pardon (Leviticus 5:1-6).

Repentance: to show remorse by feeling sorry for having participated in evil or involved in an error. It is an expression of regret for walking in disobedience.

Forgiveness: takes place after a fault has been admitted, based on confession and expression of repentance has occurred, and then we begin to ask for pardon. At this point, we recognize Jesus as our Redeemer who shed His blood to ransom us from sin.

Restitution: The experience of cleansing also brings us into making peace with those who have offended us.

Praise: As soon as we observe the process of cleansing, we feel released and renewed. And then the joy of salvation will start to flow from deep within, and we become overwhelmed. The joy of salvation will then motivate us into singing songs of praise.

Worship and Adoration: In the process of singing the songs of praise, we flow so easily into the atmosphere of worship and adoration. Of course, in His presence, it is easier to present our requests to the Lord. Even before we make our requests, the Lord begins to respond to the secret needs in our hearts through the power of revelation.

Regular Observation: We must endeavor to observe the process of cleansing every time we set out for prayer. This will give us easy access into the presence of the Lord.

Prayer Tactics (Sample)
(Remember to observe the <u>Spiritual Protocol</u>)

State the Problem:
I want to have an effective prayer life.

Prayer Focus:
Ask the Lord to teach you how to pray effectively,

- That you will be fervent and persistent in prayer
- That you will not be afraid to risk your life for a just cause
- That you will learn tactical approach to prayer.

The Authority of Scripture:
"Lord, teach us to pray . . ." (Luke 11:1).

The Prayer:
O Lord and my God, thank You for giving me life and strength.

Thank You for granting me the opportunity to learn about effective prayer.

O Lord, teach me to pray.

I submit myself to learning, that you may also teach me tactical approach to effective prayer, even as Queen Esther did in behalf of the children of Hebrew.

O Lord, like Esther, let me not be afraid to risk my life for a just cause, so that people might be set free from bondage and captivity.

Teach me to take the step of faith
when it is needed for me to make progress.

This I pray in the name of Jesus Christ our Lord and Savior. Amen.

Observations – write your experience after the prayer:

_____
_____
_____

Achievements – what did you gain from this prayer?

_____
_____
_____

Set Goals and Achievements

Having been informed about the different types of prayers that exist in the Bible and Volume I of the "School of Strategic Prayer" series, it is pertinent to set up your goals and the type of results you expect to achieve, as requested in this chapter and before you continue with this reading. This book gives you practical steps to effective prayer through warfare and confrontations. Therefore, setting up your goals is part of the tactics you need to adopt in order to pray effectively to overcome the forces of darkness.

- Do not make your prayer a traditional routine.
- Do not make your prayer an empty conversation.
- Do not let your prayer sound noisy like you are making appeal to the devil.
- Do not let your prayer sound as though you are obeying a command under duress.
- Do not let your offering be an empty barrel disturbing your peace.

List the prayer topics in order to keep you focus on the reasons you set out to pray. There is a need for you to establish your purpose.

State The Matter:	The Cause:	The Expectation:
1.		
2.		
3.		
4.		
5.		
6.		
7.		
8.		
9.		
10.		

Map out your focus:

_____
_____
_____

State your objective:
_____
_____
_____

State your aim:
_____
_____
_____

Achievements:
_____
_____
_____

Choice of Prayer Tactics

Choose the type of prayer that is suitable for your need. Each request may need a different tactical approach. You must be able to determine whether you are focusing on the prayer of thanksgiving or the prayer of intercession. That is the essence of specifying your need as required above. If you ignore any of the protocols required for each tactic, you might encounter some difficulties later in the process of your prayer, especially when it seems as though your prayers are not being answered, and you are not able to point out your achievement.

Many people usually assume that they know what is being said; and some think that they have already followed the procedure recommended in this discussion; while others believe they have made similar approach in the past but did not achieve the type of result expected. The fact is that the individuals that express such attitudes are often unteachable and do not like to take instructions from others. These categories of people think that they know, so they ignore the recommended procedures. Most of the people in these categories usually like to figure out things rather than follow instructions. Unless such people become submissive and accept and follow instructions, they will not be able to achieve their expectations.

In the preceding volume and the initial chapters of this book, sample prayers were presented at the end of each discussion to help you to modify your pattern of prayer. The sample prayer will enable you to overcome the difficulty with what to say and how to pray. In the subsequent chapters, samples of tactical and confrontational prayers will be presented in the same manner and for the same purpose.

Also, there is a portion to help you monitor the reactions that take place when you are praying, such as your feelings, perceptions and pace of the prayer. You should also monitor the change in the atmosphere. Find out if your environment gets lighter, and check if you are motivated to pray more. Also check if you got hilarious, hysterical or excited during the prayer. Whatever you discover will help you to examine your prayer focus and experiences.

Prayer Sample
(Remember to observe the Spiritual Protocol)

State the Problem:
Wisdom to identify my prayer need

Prayer Focus: Ask for wisdom for direction—

- Wisdom to understand yourself
- Wisdom to analyze your personal aims and objectives
- Wisdom to identify the purpose for every decision that you make
- Wisdom to accept instructions that will help me to achieve the purpose of life

The Authority of Scripture: Proverbs 2:1-9

The Prayer:
Blessed be the name of the Lord, the great and mighty God, the Rock of Ages. There is none like you.

My God and my Father, I have come before you to seek wisdom and direction.

O Lord, according to thy word in Proverbs 2:1-9,

Grant me wisdom to know and understand how to make decisions

And to handle the situations that confront me daily.

Teach me to seek wisdom as silver that I may understand the fear of God.

O Lord, you are the buckler to them that walk uprightly.

Therefore, grant me wisdom to make decisions that are pleasing unto you.

Direct my path that I may walk in your light. Amen!

Observations – write your experience after the prayer:

_____
_____
_____

Achievements – what did you gain from this prayer?

CHAPTER TWO

The Purpose of Warfare Prayer

—∞—

There are so many reasons why we go to war. We go to war to confront the enemy against harassment and spiritual terrorism. We go to war to take back what the enemy has stolen from us. We go to war to repossess our wealth. We go to war to establish our legal grounds. We go to war to strengthen our authority. We go to war to establish our strongholds. Therefore, in order to conquer the enemy and win your wars, you need to be properly equipped by mapping out your targets adequately (Genesis 14:13-16).

Setting Your Goals

Similarly, in order to win your spiritual wars, you first of all need to set out your goals that will help you to pray effectively. You also need to your presentations clear and simple as indicated in Chapter One.

Preparing Your Agenda

- Prepare your agenda tactfully.
- Be determined to achieve your set goal.
- Plan to win the battle against the enemy.
- Do not work with assumption.
- Avoid propounding theories or logics that have not been tested.
- Deal with actuality if you really want to achieve practical results.

If you are realistic with your presentations, you would also achieve workable results that would practically change your life for good, and your prayer life would never be the same again. Amen!

Sample Prayer
(Remember to observe the <u>Spiritual Protocol</u>)

State the Problem:
Teach me to war against the enemy.

Prayer Focus:
Lord, make me a soldier and also teach me to confront the enemy.

The Authority of Scripture: 1 Samuel 30:1-10

The Prayer:
Praise to the Holiest in the Highest.
Glory be to His holy name,
For Jehovah God is the man of war who conquers the enemy
And gives me victory
O Lord, I ask that You will train me to be a Christian soldier.
Equip me with the weapons of warfare.
Teach my hands to make war against the foe.
When the enemy confronts me, teach me to inquire of You
As David did, and help me to abide by Your instructions,
So that You will direct my ways on the battlefield.
This I pray in the name of Jesus Christ our Lord. Amen!

Observations – write your experience after the prayer:

_____
_____
_____

Achievements – what did you gain from this prayer?

_____
_____
_____

CHAPTER THREE

The War of Eviction

Evicting demons is a war against Satan. It is a militant approach to prayer. You cannot evict demons by offering a quiet prayer, but rather with an aggressive one. Satan is always at war with Christians, as he tries to take both the offensive and defensive to repossess the body from which his cohorts have been evicted.

After they have been evicted, demons do not accept defeat, they struggle and fight for repossession. They try to claim legal grounds for legal occupancy. Eviction is an intense war that causes interference in prayer for individuals involved. Demons can frustrate people out of prayer or weaken their prayer life. They frustrate people from enjoying prayer sessions by making individuals to lose interest or feel it is not necessary to spend quality time with God. The demons influence people to assume that God knows all things and understands their excuses.

Demons also weaken an individual's prayer life with fatigue and drowsiness. Individuals are distracted with unnecessary issues that can wait for another time. Do not allow matters that are not spiritual to compete with your prayer time. It is dangerous to take your prayer time for granted.

Jesus said in Matthew 12:43-45 that,

When an unclean spirit goes out of a man, he goes through dry places, seeking rest, and finds none. Then he says, "<u>I will return to my house from which I came</u>." And when he comes, he finds it empty, swept, and put in order. <u>Then he goes and takes with him seven other spirits more wicked than himself, and they enter and dwell there</u>; and the last state of that man is worse than the first. So shall it also be with this wicked generation. (Emphasis added)

Prayer Tactics
(Remember to observe the <u>Spiritual Protocol</u>)

State the Problem:
You have asked the Lord to equip you for warfare. Confront the enemy, and evict the evil spirits.

Prayer Focus:
To be aggressive in your confrontation against the enemy

- To keep your fire burning so that what has been ejected will not return
- To avoid doing things that will attract demonic interferences

The Authority of Scripture: Matthew 12:43-45

The Prayer of Confrontation:
Jesus, I thank you for dying on the cross to redeem me from my sins and deliver me from evil.

Glory be to your precious name.

Thank you also for giving me your precious name to war against the devil.

Your name is power and authority against Satan.

At the mention of your name, every knee shall bow and every tongue shall confess that indeed, Jesus is Lord.

Because of the authority in your name,

I stand to rebuke the devil and to raise a standard against the workers of iniquity this day.

Hey, Satan, I come against you in the name of Jesus.

I confront you with the authority in the blood of Jesus and I raise a standard against your cohorts.

With the authority in the name of Jesus, I evict you from my life and out of my environment.

You have no legal authority over me,

Because Jesus is Lord over my life.

You cannot control me,

Because I have been washed by the blood of Jesus.

With the authority in the name of Jesus, I command you to go away from me right now.

You shall not return unto me again,

And I shall not give you access into my life,

Because the Word of God says that,

He who the Son of God sets free, shall be free indeed.

Therefore, I claim my freedom from you in the name of Jesus.

Go out of my life, out of my soul, out of my body and out of my spirit.

The blood of Jesus builds a wall between you and me.

You shall not see me again, and I shall also not invite you.

In Jesus' name, I evict you demons

and claim my total freedom in the blood of Jesus. Amen.

Observations – write your experience after the prayer:

_____

_____

_____

Achievements – what did you gain from this prayer?

_____

_____

_____

CHAPTER FOUR

Specific Prayer

Warfare is not a general prayer, but a specific prayer. It is a process of addressing specific issues that affect you. To address the issue that bothers your life, you must open your mouth and confront the devil on a specific matter and expect the devil to react in a specific manner. Do not generalize the activities of the enemy, and do not give demons a general instruction.

If you have been suffering frequent accidents, do not go before Satan and say, "I bind you in the name of Jesus." Nothing will happen. You need to address the spirit that causes accidents by saying, "In the name of Jesus I command you spirit of accident to go away from me." Then the spirit of accident will hear it being addressed and commanded to go. Of course it will obey you because of the authority in the name of Jesus Christ.

Specific prayer will help you keep a focused on what your needs are and what you actually mean to say. Therefore, you will be able to hear and understand what God might be saying to you. Many people ignore God's instruction and direction that come as a response to their prayers, because they were neither focused nor specific in their utterances. Some revelations seem weird and meaningless to us because we lack focus and specifics. Daniel was very focused and specific in prayer, so he was able to understand the revelations that God showed him (Daniel 10:12).

Prayer Tactics
(Remember to observe the Spiritual Protocol)

State the Problem:
To overcome the evil spirits that torment me in my sleep.

The Problem:
You have been under spiritual torment, whereby demons try to embarrass you in public. The demons have been harassing you in your home and in your sleep.

Prayer Focus:
Open your mouth and rebuke the spiritual terrorists. Command them not to perform a specific operation in your life (*mention what they have been doing to you*).

- Command them to stop harassing you in your home and sleep.

- Command them not to embarrass you anymore.

The Authority of Scripture: John 1:4-5; Psalm 91

The Prayer:
Lord Jesus, thank you for giving me the power and authority to confront the enemy of my life.

Because of Your power and presence, in the name of Jesus I release myself from all manner of demonic contamination.

Hey, Satan, listen to me.

Jesus died on the cross to buy my pardon

And to redeem me by the blood that He shed on the cross.

I have been washed by the blood of Jesus

I recognize the blood of Jesus is against you.

The Scripture declares in John 1:4-5 that, "In Him was life, and the life was the light of men. The light shines in the darkness, and the darkness did not comprehend it."

Light has come, therefore darkness must go.

Therefore, no demon shall terrorize my life in the name of Jesus.

In the name of Jesus, let the spirit of darkness go out of my life right now.

I stand in the blood of Jesus to declare that

Evil spirits shall no longer come after me by any means.

With the authority in the blood of Jesus,

I command you to stop following me around.

Stop embarrassing me, for the light of God has come.

In the name of Jesus, stop interfering with my sleep.

You shall not come close to my residence,

For Jesus Christ is the light of my life.

Therefore, in the name of Jesus, you shall not enter my home.

There is no accommodation for you in this place.

Go away from me, for the word of God is against you,

And the blood of Jesus is also against you.

You have been defeated on the cross of Calvary.

Go out of my life, out of my soul, out of my body, out of my spirit,

Out of my environment, out of my home.

You shall no longer be my guest nor my host.

You shall not be my guide, nor shall you give me any false protection.

The blood of Jesus builds a wall of protection around me.

I command you, spirit of darkness,

To go to the "dead sea" and remain there until your judgment day

In Jesus' name I pray. Amen.

Observations – write your experience after the prayer:

_____
_____
_____

Achievements – what did you gain from this prayer?

_____
_____
_____

CHAPTER FIVE

Standing on Scriptures

It is very crucial that the prayer of warfare must be made with Scriptural references. The devil has no respect for people who have no knowledge of Scripture. You do not have any authority in yourself to confront the enemy. You are powerless without the Word of God. The Word of God is the sword of the Spirit. It is the weapon of our warfare. Therefore, do not go to war against the devil with logic or intellectual ability. You will be wounded very badly, and that may weaken your faith and discourage your Christian life.

When Satan tried to offend Jesus after a 40-day fast, Jesus resisted him by making Scriptural references. Thus Jesus stood on the Word of God to overcome the temptations of the enemy (Matthew 4:1-11).

Recently I ministered to a lady who was being terrorized by evil spirits. The demons claim the representatives of her forefathers from territory. The demons mentioned her parents' name and made references to certain incidents that took place during her childhood. This made her believe that the demons were actually on special errands. One of their missions was to prevent her from attending a charismatic church where deliverance ministration takes place. They told her not to go to a specific denomination where she has been undergoing counseling and deliverance ministration. They also instructed her to attend a particular denomination where they will not be exposed.

When I came into contact with her, I noticed that she had not been studying the Scriptures, and this had made it impossible for the demons to stay away from her. Anytime the evil spirits were cast out, they returned to her as soon as she entered her residence. The demons always left but went nowhere but to her home. She heard their voices as they spoke to her in familiar voices of family members.

Before I started her ministration, I introduced her to Scripture reading. I instructed her to spend hours reading aloud to her own hearing. As she read the Scriptures, the demons exited. She practically saw the demons go away. Then it happened that when she recovered, she stopped attending midweek Bible studies, and she also stopped studying the Scriptures. Of course the demons returned and her situation became worse than ever before (Matthew 12: 43-45). She was in torment for another whole year until I returned to that city again. Immediately, when I saw her, I discerned her state of torment. When I started to interview her, she began to manifest.

This time I asked her to stay up all night reading the Scriptures and also to play the Bible on tape 24 hours everyday. This would make her home and body uncomfortable for the demons to come close or to terrorize her life. When the Bible on cassette began to play, there was commotion in the house. She practically heard the demons screaming and rushing out "Let's go, let's go. We can't stay here anymore." At the same time, her body also trembled for a while and she felt very light. Then the joy of the Lord filled her soul, and she started to laugh and worship the Lord as never before. Now she is free because of the Word of God.

Even when we present a prayer request before the Lord, we need to do so on the basis of the Word of God. When God wanted to eliminate the children of Israel in the wilderness because of their stubbornness, Moses reminded God about His promises to Abraham, Isaac and Jacob (Exodus 32:12-13).

We have the promise of the Father to stand on Biblical truth to convince God to manifest His Word by giving us victory over the enemy of our faith, as stated in Isaiah 45:11 – "Thus says the Lord, The Holy One of Israel, and his Maker: 'Ask Me of things to come concerning My sons, and concerning the work of My hands, you command Me.'"

The Prince of Persia withheld Daniel's prayer and would not allow the angel Gabriel to pass through, so the angel Michael had to come and fight the war against the principalities of darkness. Angel Gabriel is the messenger that carries the message of joy and peace to earth. Angel Michael is the warrior that fights battles on behalf of the saints.

Prayer Tactics
(Remember to observe the Spiritual Protocol)

State the Problem:

You have been hearing voices giving you instructions, and you have always associated what you hear with God, but after a while you receive another instruction, yet nothing is happening. Meanwhile, things are getting worse and you are frustrated.

- You need to rebuke the interfering voices with the Scriptures.
- You need to cast out the controlling spirits that have been giving the conflicting instructions.
- You need the knowledge of Scripture to pray aright.

Prayer Focus:

Use Scriptures as the sword of the Spirit against the foe.

- Declare what the Word of God says and what it means to you.
- Insist that there is power in the Word of God.
- Command the controlling spirits to stop instructing you.

- Command the controlling spirits to stop dictating the pace of your life.
- Rebuke the demons from coming close to you.
- Build a wall of protection around your ears with the blood of Jesus.
- Seal your ears with the Word of God so that you will not hear interfering voices, but the Scriptural truth.

The Authority of Scripture: Isaiah 45:11

The Prayer:

Thank You, Jesus, for the Word of Truth.

Chapter one of the book of John states that, "In the beginning was the Word, and the Word was with God, and the Word was God."

The Word of God also declares that, "He was in the beginning with God. All things were made through Him, and without Him nothing was made that was made."

Therefore, I declare the Word of God into my body, soul and spirit, and I say to you demons, you cannot possess my body nor control me because I am created by the Word of God, and I exist by the power of creation.

The Word of God is the power of the spoken word, and I am created by the word that God spoke into being.

I shall hear no other voice but the voice of God.

I shall heed no other instruction but the commands of the Lord.

Yes, I declare the Word of God as it was in the beginning into my ears and on my lips.

Satan, I overcome you by the Word of God,

Go away from me in the name of Jesus.

With the authority in the blood of Jesus, I rebuke you,

You shall no longer speak to me, and I shall not hear your voice anymore.

Go out of my thoughts, out of my imagination, out of my mind and out of my ears.

I release the blood of Jesus to seal my ears from hearing you demonic voices.

I release the Word of God to surround me and fill my heart, soul and body in the name of Jesus.

Thank You, Lord, for Your Word is power and authority.

Thank You for giving me Your Word as a wall of protection around my life.

This I pray in the name of Jesus Christ my Lord and Savior. Amen.

Observations – write your experience after the prayer:

_____
_____
_____

Achievements – what did you gain from this prayer?

_____
_____
_____

CHAPTER SIX

Speaking with Knowledge and Authority

As Christian soldiers, we have to learn to open our mouths and speak out the Word of God with boldness and confidence against the foe. When we open our mouths to chew the Word, the words of our mouths will be enriched with the gospel of truth. In times of war, the Word of God will then become like a two edged sword in our mouths. The Word will also become fire against the enemy. We would also be confident to open our mouths to spit fire against the enemy. Jesus said in John 12:49, "For I have not spoken on My own authority; but the Father who sent Me gave Me a command, what I should say and what I should speak."

Opening our mouths to speak out is very vital in warfare. We open our mouths for several reasons—to bless or curse. Blessing is an act of pronouncing a goodwill message in the name of the Lord or imparting a divine or spiritual favor upon a person, while cursing is a negative statement uttered to harm or do evil. Cursing is also a swear word or evil spell cast on people to inflict suffering or punishment on them. Number 22:35 states that, "Then the Angel of the LORD said to Balaam, 'Go with the man, but only the word that I speak to you, that you shall speak.'"

Balaam opened his mouth to bless the children of Israel when he had actually been hired to curse them. Balak wanted to hear Balaam make the evil pronouncements, but Balak rather heard a positive declaration. There is power in the spoken word; that is why Balak could not curse the Israelite himself but needed someone with a stronger and unique authority to speak out the curse. Number 22:6 says,

Therefore, please come at once, <u>curse this people for me, for they are too mighty for me. Perhaps I shall be able to defeat them</u> and drive them out of the land, for I know that he whom you bless is blessed, and he whom you curse is cursed. (Emphasis added)

In view of divine intervention, Balaam rather made unique and positive pronouncement to uplift Israel while Israel's enemy was cursed. Numbers 23:20, 23-24 says,

Behold, I have received a command to bless; He has blessed, and I cannot reverse it.

> **...For there is no sorcery against Jacob,**
> **Nor any divination against Israel;**
> **It now must be said of Jacob**
> **And of Israel,**
> **"Oh, what God has done!"**
> **Look, a people rises like a lioness,**
> **And lifts itself up like a lion;**
> **It shall not lie down until it devours the prey,**
> **And drinks the blood of the slain."**

This pronouncement from Numbers 23:20-24 was a declaration of victory over the enemy of Israel. Balak was defeated at the hearing of this word and went home disappointed. The words of our mouths do reflect the state of our hearts. When we study the Scripture, we invest spiritual wealth into our spirits, and when we read occult books, we amass evil into our spirits.

The purpose of warfare is to win a battle against the enemy. The word of our mouths can be powerful and daring for the enemy.

Prayer Tactics
(Remember to observe the <u>Spiritual Protocol</u>)

State the Problem:

There are indications that you or members of your family have been cursed. If there are problems in the family that have spanned from generation to generation, if there are persistent problems in your family or your personal life, then, it is obvious that you have either inherited a curse or your own action or behavior has attracted a curse. In view of this observation or problem, you need to break the curse if it is just you. But if it has to do with the whole family, then you need to uproot the whole tree (See my book on *Pulling down Satanic Strongholds* for details).

Prayer Focus:

Break the curses you have noted in your family and the recurrent problems in your life.

Use as many Bible passages as possible to defend yourself as you uproot the curses.

Be specific if you must achieve results.

Specific prayer will yield specific results.

Uproot the following:

- Curses in the family
- Curses in your own life
- Recurring problems

The Authority of Scripture: Numbers 23:23

The Prayer:

Thank You, Lord, for Your Word that gives us power and authority over the enemy.

Thank You because by Your Word the power of darkness is broken, and we are able to receive freedom and liberty in Jesus' name.

With the authority in the name of Jesus,

In the name of Jesus, I command you, Satan, to listen to the Word of God, any evil that was once planted into my life will never prevail.

In the name of Jesus, the generational curses that exist in my family will no longer manifest in my life, nor prevail against me.

The Word of God declares that Jesus died on the cross to take away my sins.

Therefore, my sins have been washed away by the blood of Jesus.

The Scripture declares in Number 23:20a, 23 that "He has blessed, and I cannot reverse it . . . For there is no sorcery against Jacob, Nor any divination against Israel." Therefore, I declare that God has blessed me, and no one can curse me.

In the name of Jesus there shall be no enchantment against my family and myself.

Devil, I insist that God has blessed me, and no one can curse me.

Therefore, I uproot the trees of curses planted over my head, my life, my home and my family.

In the name of Jesus, I command the trees of evil to be uprooted right now.

With the authority in the blood of Jesus,

I command fire to consume the root of the evil tree that ever existed in my life.

I declare that the curses from the forefathers shall no longer set my teeth on edge.

Because of the blood of Jesus I shall not inherit the sins of the fathers; neither would I pay for their sins,nor inherit their woes. Jesus has paid for my sins, therefore I am not entitled to bear that burden anymore.

The blood of Jesus is sufficient for me.

Thank You, Lord, for the blood.

Thank you for buying my pardon.

For there shall be no enchantment against me and my family.

God has blessed us, and no one can curse us.

Therefore, we reject any curse directed to us,

And in Jesus' name, we ask the fire of the Holy Spirit to consume the curses.

Amen!

Observations – write your experience after the prayer:

_____
_____
_____

Achievements – what did you gain from this prayer?

_____
_____
_____

CHAPTER SEVEN

War of Words

Spiritual warfare is a war of words. It is a war in which the power of the spoken word is used as a weapon against the foe. Words are powerful and can be either healing or demoralizing to a hearer. For instance, in ordinary life, rebuke is a type of correction that simply means stop. However, in the spiritual realm rebuke is an utterance that is used to weaken an opponent's ability to perform or excel. In fact, rebuke is a weapon of demoralization against the foe.

In the war between Israel and the Philistines, for 40 days and nights, Goliath frightened the children of Israel with a war of words, so much so that Israel was demoralized and afraid to get into the battlefield to face the enemy. Goliath did not use ordinary words but swear words and curses as indicated in 1 Samuel 17: 8-10:

> **Then he stood and cried out to the armies of Israel, and said to them, "Why have you**

come out to line up for battle? Am I not a Philistine, and you the servants of Saul? Choose a man for yourselves, and let him come down to me. If he is able to fight with me and kill me, then we will be your servants. But if I prevail against him and kill him, then you shall be our servants and serve us." And the Philistine said, "I defy the armies of Israel this day, give me a man, that we may fight together."

When Saul and the army of Israel heard the words of the Philistine giant, 1 Samuel 17:11 says, ". . . they were dismayed and greatly afraid." But when young and youthful David heard the foul utterances of the Philistine champion defying Israel, he was stirred up to challenge Goliath. Therefore, David responded on behalf of Israel in 1 Samuel 17:26:

"What shall be done for the man who kills this Philistine, and takes away the reproach from Israel? For who is this uncircumcised Philistine, that he should defy the armies of the living God?"

Just like the words of the Philistine giant had frightened and demoralized Israel's army, also the words of young David stirred up some courage in the hearts of the Israelites, so that David's words of encouragement were reported to King Saul and he sent for him. David encouraged King Saul in 1 Samuel

17:32, "Let no man's heart fail because of him; your servant will go and fight with this Philistine."

Although Saul seemed to be encouraged, he had not overcome the impact of the utterances made by the Philistine champion. He was still gripped with fear and self-defeat. As a result, he tried to discourage David at the same level. King Saul said to David in verse 33: "You are not able to go against this Philistine to fight with him: for you are a youth, and he a man of war from his youth."

The fear entertained by King Saul would not affect young David, who was also a warrior in the wilderness among lions and bears. So David would not accept the venom of defeat from the king, but rather presented his heroic records in retrospect, 1 Samuel 17:36-37 states:

Your servant has killed both lion and bear; and this uncircumcised Philistine will be like one of them, seeing he has defied the armies of the living God. ...The LORD, who delivered me from the paw of the lion and from the paw of the bear, He will deliver me from the hand of this Philistine.

When David was approaching Goliath, the giant started to rebuke and disdain him with a war of words so that David would be weakened and frightened to get close. But the more the Philistine giant made his harassments, the more David gathered boldness and confidence to face him. When the Philistine noticed that David would not be moved by his foul language, he rained more curses but to no avail. 1 Samuel 17:43-44,

> **So the Philistine said to David, "Am I a dog, that you come to me with sticks?" And the Philistine cursed David by his gods. And the Philistine said to David, "Come to me, and I will give your flesh to the birds of the air and the beasts of the field!"**

Instead, David also drew from His wealth of knowledge about Jehovah God from Scriptures and responded that the battle is the Lord's (vv. 45-47 Emphasis added).

> **Then David said to the Philistine, "You come to me with a sword, with a spear, and with a javelin. <u>But I come to you in the name of the LORD of hosts</u>, the God of the armies of Israel, whom you have defied. This day the LORD will deliver you into my hand, and I will strike you and take your head from you. And this day I will give the carcasses of the camp of the Philistines to the birds of the air and the wild beasts of the earth, that all the earth may know that there is a God in Israel. Then all this assembly shall know <u>that the LORD does not save with sword and spear; for the battle is the LORD's,</u> and He will give you into our hands."**

By making such a remark, David reversed the curse that Goliath had put on the armies of Israel, and the curse became a pruninghook against the Philistines (v. 50).

So David prevailed over the Philistine with a sling and a stone, and struck the Philistine and killed him. But there was no sword in the hand of David.

Therefore, the battle started with a war of words before it mounted up to the use of weaponry and ended up with physical combat and slaughter of the enemy. Indeed, the war of words is a battlefield.

When I was a sports journalist, I noticed that most boxers and wrestlers use the war of words to demoralize their opponents even before they enter the ring. Some fighters lose the battle, not because they do not have the ability to fight, but because the opponent has sent them "satanic verses" and 'spiritual missiles' through word of mouth. After losing a fight against Lennox Lewis of England, Mike Tyson of America announced that he would eat the heart of Lewis. Before then, Tyson had bitten the ear of Evander Hollyfield in a boxing ring.

Even on the football field and in the basketball court, athletes harass and bully one another with the use of foul language in order to demoralize their opponents. Similarly, spectators on the sidelines do worse, as they bully by painting their opponent with satanic pictures and swear words. Likewise, politicians use a war of words to harass and terrorize their opposition parties.

Indeed, the war of words is nothing less than an insult rained upon an opponent or enemy in order to conquer or overcome that competitive opponent or enemy through psychological intimidation. The war of words becomes psychological weapons of depression, oppression, suppression and frustration that afflict the mental state of a person's life.

Prayer Tactics
(Remember to observe the Spiritual Protocol)

State the Problem:

Oftentimes, certain individuals make negative pronouncements over your life that you did not know how to reject. Some of the pronouncements are very devastating and depressing. If you have been demoralized by the negative pronouncements that have been spoken to you, then you need to reject those words and break the impact that they made over your life.

If the conversations you hear often trouble your mind and heart, and give you heart pain, hurt, confusion, depression or rejection, then you need to fight against the spirit controlling them. There is an evil spirit responsible for inciting negative activities against you.

Prayer Focus:
Pray that the Lord would help you to decipher between words that ignite blessings and words that invoke curses—

- That Satan will no longer use anyone against you
- That Satan will no longer incite others to throw words of destruction at you
- Rebuke that spirit of rejection, and call forth the spirit of acceptance into your body, soul and spirit.
- Call on the spirit of favor and love to surround you, so that whoever sees you will bless and encourage you.
- Uproot the negatives from your life and plant the positives (*mention the negative things in your life*).
- Uproot the curses and replace them with blessings (*mention the curses in your life*).

The Authority of Scripture: 1 Samuel 17:50

The Prayer:
You are worthy, O Lord, to receive glory, honor and adoration. You are the Rock of Ages, the Mighty Warrior in Battle.

Lord Jesus, I come before Your presence to ask for wisdom of words to wage war against the battle of life,

That I may know the difference between words that ignite blessings and words that invoke curses.

O Lord, turn the words of my mouth into blessings, that I would always bless the people of God, so that I may also enjoy Your blessings.

Teach me to use Your Word as a weapon of warfare against the enemy of my soul, even as David used Your Word against the Philistines in the book of 1 Samuel 17, until foes are defeated. Amen!

Prayer of Confrontation:

Hey, Satan, you are a defeated foe.

Jesus defeated you on the cross at Calvary over 2000 years ago.

You are a coward and a loser, therefore you dare not touch me because of the blood of Jesus Christ that was shed for me.

Listen, Satan, the Word of God is sharper than two edged sword, piercing through bones and marrows and tearing asunder every work of iniquity.

Therefore, I come against you with the Word of the Lord in the name of Jesus.

The Word of God says God has blessed me and no one can curse me.

Therefore, I reject any negative word that is uttered against me in the spiritual realm and in the physical realm.

With the authority in the blood of Jesus, I reverse any curse invoked with my image in the name of Jesus.

The Word of God says there shall be no divination against Jacob, therefore I declare in the name of Jesus that there shall be no enchantment against me.

I command in the name of Jesus any enchantment directed towards me to be consumed by fire.

In Jesus name, I reverse any curse directed towards me in Jesus name.

Observations – write your experience after the prayer:

_____
_____
_____

Achievements – what did you gain from this prayer?

_____
_____
_____

CHAPTER EIGHT

Difficulties and Interferences

There are several reasons why individual churchgoers are not able to spend hours in prayer. The reasons are numerous and could be overwhelming, yet they are issues that need crucial attention if one actually wants to enjoy fellowship with the divine. The reasons could be difficulties that relate to our backgrounds and associations, especially on the side of our family traits.

Difficulties in prayer could be as a result of our personal misgivings and weaknesses, while interference could be caused by relationship traits. However, spiritual interference is usually caused by our past and present involvement in mysticism and spiritualism. Indulgence in any form of spirituality outside of the Christian faith is an open door for evil infiltration into our minds, souls and spirits. Besides, indulgences in mysticism and spirituality might have involved a soul-tie or a blood covenant. Unless the bond is broken, the evil spirits involved in the covenant will continue to hang around. (See my book, *Pulling Down Satanic Strongholds* for details on Interfering Spirits).

Prayer Tactics
(Remember to observe the Spiritual Protocol)

State the Problem:
Need to discover the cause of the difficulties in my life.

Prayer Focus:
Breaking covenants made ignorantly.

- Renouncing soul-ties
- Renouncing past involvement in mysticism or spiritualism.

The Authority of Scripture: Leviticus 19:26-28

The Prayer:
Precious Savior, thank you for your love and care over my life.
Thank you for giving me a revelation concerning the difficulties I need to tackle in my life.
Father God, You are my Lord and my Creator.
You are the God of yesterday, today and forever.
My life and destiny is in Your hands.
You are the potter and I am the clay.
Break me, melt me and remold me, and fill me with Your spirit.

Grant me wisdom, knowledge and understanding to overcome the tides of life,

So that I will not be overwhelmed by the challenges that confront my endeavors.

Help me to trust You and Your power of creation.

You are the God that makes the impossible to become possible.

Therefore, with You all things are possible.

Thank You for sorting me out and delivering me from evil.

The Confrontation:

In the name of Jesus, and with the authority in the blood of Jesus, I come against all manner of interfering spirits confronting my life with challenges.

In the name of Jesus, I renounce all past relationships with the occult.

I release myself from vows or covenants made with demonic entities in the spiritual realm and in the physical realm.

The blood of Jesus nullifies the consequences of the demonic covenants in my life.

With the authority in the blood of Jesus, I uproot any tree of evil planted over my life that is bearing briers and thorns in my life.

With the authority in the blood of Jesus, I command the trees of evil in my life to be uprooted and consumed by fire.

With the authority in the blood of Jesus, I restrain the arrows of the enemy from touching me.

Strategic Prayer Tactics II

In the name of Jesus, I command the fire of the Holy Ghost to consume the arrows that fly by day and the terrors by night.

Jesus is Lord over my life.

There is power in the blood of Jesus, and the blood of Jesus is sufficient for me.

Thank You, Lord, for delivering me from evil.

Praise God from whom all blessings flow.

This I pray in the name of Jesus. Amen.

Observations – write your experience after the prayer:

_____
_____
_____

Achievements – what did you gain from this prayer?

_____
_____
_____

CHAPTER NINE

Legal Grounds

Legal ground is the official or fundamental authority that an individual has over an issue, a place, a property, a document, a people, a relationship, a territory, a possession, or information. It is a process of having a lawful access to a possession. Legal ground gives an individual a lawful authority to operate in a place or to take charge of an affair.

There is certain information that needs to be put right so that a person can confidently declare his/her legal authority over the enemy. We need to be aware of the details of names and how we came by them. The names we bear could bring legal implications in both the spiritual and physical realms. When a name has a spiritual implication, then it is likely that a person will be affected in the physical and secular realm. (For more details, check my book on *When Satan Went to Church*).

Identity Card

Our spiritual birth gives us a legal identity in Christ Jesus and legal belonging to the body of Christ. It also gives us access into the Kingdom of God. The date and occasion we confessed and accepted Jesus Christ into our lives as our Lord and Savior is a legal identity against Satan and his cohorts. Our spiritual birth is connected to the crucifixion of Jesus Christ—the shedding of His blood and His death on the cross. (See details in Chapter Thirteen.)

Illegal Possessions

If you are a regenerated or born again Christian, and you have items that belong to the kingdom of darkness in your possession, the enemy will have a legal access into your life. When Satan gives you a possession, he also gives you a mark of identity, which is a sense of belonging. Therefore, if you decide to withdraw from his camp, then you also need to give up his properties. You might have to go through the process of deliverance ministration to break the alliance and satanic identity in your life so that you obtain freedom from satanic interferences.

Indulgence and Diabolism

If you used to indulge in diabolic activities or consult satanic agents for some sort of assistance before you gave your life to Christ, then it is likely that you bear a demonic identity that gives Satan and his cohort legal access into your life, home, and family endeavors. It is important that you seek special attention to break the spiritual link; otherwise you will suffer spiritual harassment and terrorism from demonic realms. In case you have made some vows or covenants to satanic agents (human hosts or representatives) you will also need to renounce and break the vows and covenants in order to receive total release.

Illegal Open Doors

If you are a Christian and you visit a prayer house where a satanic host operates, then you have opened your doors to illegal activities in your life. If you indulge in psychic, palm reading, zodiac and horoscope activities, you are operating on satanic legal grounds. Such indulgence is an open door to satanic interferences. Satan and his cohorts will have the freedom to access your life at anytime. When you go to church, they cause you to sleep during the sermon. You will be weak during prayer and will be lazy to read your Bible.

You may have a huge interest in the things of God, but the enemy will hinder you from the wealth of legal stability in the Kingdom of God.

The subsequent chapters will discuss various avenues through which legal and illegal doors are opened and closed up in our lives. The legal grounds discussed include: Names, Addresses, Biological and Spiritual Births and relationships.

Prayer Tactics
(Remember to observe the Spiritual Protocol)

State the Problem:
You are in possession of an item that does not belong to you, and you are yet to seek for permission from the rightful owner, hence you have been experiencing some form of interference in your life. Unfortunately, you were not conscious of the fact that you have been operating on illegal grounds until now.

Prayer Focus:
Need to repent over the illegal possession of the item in your possession.

- Need to renounce the interferences you are experiencing.
- Need to rebuke the enemy for harassing you.

The Authority of Scripture: 1 Samuel 13:8-14

The Prayer:
Lord Jesus, I come before your throne just as I am to repent of my sins. I have acted illegally and have opened my doors to the enemy to plunder me.

I ask for forgiveness of sin even as I repent right now.

I ask that the blood of Jesus will wash and cleanse me from my iniquity, and in the name of Jesus release me from all manner of entanglement.

Prayer of Confrontation:

Satan, I come against you in the name of Jesus.

You shall no longer interfere with me because of the item in my possession.

This day, I have discovered why you had the opportunity to come in and plunder me.

I have repented and the Lord has forgiven me.

I have also been washed and set free by the blood of Jesus.

Therefore, in Jesus' name, you shall no longer frustrate me.

Go out of my life, out of my soul, out of my spirit in the name of Jesus.

The blood of Jesus builds a wall around me.

You shall not see me again, and I shall not invite you by any means.

In the name of Jesus I declare my victory. Amen.

Observations – write your experience after the prayer:

_____
_____
_____

Achievements – what did you gain from this prayer?

_____
_____
_____

CHAPTER TEN

Names

—⚌—

Name (First Name, Middle Name, Surname, Spouse Name, Father's Name, Mother's Name and Ancestor's Name): You need to find out the source of your name and its meaning.

- Were you named after somebody somewhere, and for what reason or purpose?
- What is the significance of your name and what did your parents intend to achieve, or what did they derive from that name?
- How has that name affected your life, and what impact has it made on your life?
- Are you happy to bear that name, or have you ever felt like changing your name?

This is not just your first name, but especially your surname may be a snare to you. It may carry a stigma or a curse, or even the meaning of that name might be causing you a nightmare. You need to disassociate yourself from any mystical impact to which your name may be connected.

Remembering the Dead

If you are named after a person who is dead for the sake of remembrance, you would need to pray over that name so that the "spirit of the dead" will not control the living. Otherwise the spirit of the dead will become a guide and will also give false protection to the individual concerned. Demons will take advantage of the person and begin to harass or terrorize one's life in dreams or through other means. The failure of the dead can be a controlling authority over such a person because of the name.

Haunted Names

We once ministered to an individual whose full name had a demonic impact. The demons would not leave this person alone until the name was changed. The spirit of the forefathers kept showing up to interfere with her whenever she was addressed by that name. The spirits claimed that they come under torment when those names were mentioned in the church, especially during deliverance ministration.

Inheritance for Transference

Naming a child after somebody or a situation or place may lead to transference of spirit, spiritual inheritance or a kind of impartation. In the case of transference of spirit, the force that controls the primary person whom a child is named after would automatically be transferred to that innocent child.

Hence that child would likely have strong spiritual affiliation with that personality. If the principal person is involved in occult or diabolical activities, the child is likely to indulge in the same pattern of lifestyle because of the spiritual link.

An individual once came to us crying for help. "Our son is doing the same thing that one of the parents did, and now the whole family is ruined." Then I asked, "Is the son named after one of the parents?" Of course, that was the first link for interference because the young man confessed that the parent had always said, even when he dies, his spirit will be alive because he will come back and live in his son." This is an evil impartation that is a strong interference with the image and destiny of the young man.

Transference of Spirit by Name

In another case, a grandmother, who was dying, decided to breathe out into the face of a granddaughter who was named after her. Guess what! After her death, the image of the child changed into that of her grandmother. Her voice became mature and her facial expression became like that of her late grandmother. The child began to exhibit weird behaviors that reflected the characteristics of her grandmother who was dead.

In another case, the teenage girl was a committed Christian who understood the impact of her name, so she was able to resist the grandmother's spirit. In fact, the teenager rebuked and overcame the evil spirit from her grandmother. When the grandmother died, the evil spirit of the dead tried to lure the teenager with gift items in her dreams, but the girl refused and prayed until the interferences stopped.

Biblical Names

In the Scriptures the name Jabez meant "child of sorrow" because he was born in pain. Jabez prayed and asked the Lord to deliver him from evil that he may not cause pain, *"Oh, that you would bless me indeed . . ."* (1 Chronicles 4:9-10). Also the name Ichabod means *"the glory of God has departed"* (1 Samuel 4:19-22). This was a repercussion of sin in Eli's home and the land of Israel. What is your name and what is about that name? Do not pick up a name because it is simply mentioned in the Bible. You must study the importance and implication that certain names had on the personalities involved.

In deliverance ministration, we have often used names as the first point of contact to break demonic covenants from people's lives. Surnames have been a point of contact for transference of generational curses and mishaps in families' and individual's lives. It is important that you purify your family name by the use of the blood of Jesus Christ. If the meaning of that name is connected to demonic gods, then it is better to change it. Names are powerful. Release your name from demonic access and separate it from contamination.

Prayer Tactics
(Remember to observe the <u>Spiritual Protocol</u>)

State the Problem:
Wherever your name is mentioned, there is a problem. You need to remove the stigma off your name and legalize it with the blood of Jesus so that you will no longer suffer defilement.

Prayer Focus:
What is your name?

- What is the meaning?
- What is the motive behind your bearing that name?
- What do your parents intend to achieve from that name?
- Are you named after the dead or the living?
- Are you named after a place or an image?
- Does your name affect you positively or negatively?
- Ask the Lord to reveal the intent of your name to you.
- Ask the Lord to show you if there is any demonic implication attached to your name.
- Renounce any curse attached to your name.
- Renounce the stigma or omen that influence your name.
- Pronounce blessings upon your name.

The Authority of Scripture: 1 Samuel 4:19-22 and 1 Chronicles 4:9-10

The Prayer:

O Lord and my God, my refuge and my fortress,

Thank You for bringing me into realizing the impact of my name.

O Lord, deliver me from any demonic attachment that affects my name.

Release me from all manner of curses that affect my name.

Let no evil spirit torment me again because of my name.

Change my name to blessings and cause me to prosper.

Enable me to do that which I have not been able to do because of my name; and cause this name to begin to make impact in my life.

O Lord, from today, wherever my name is mentioned, let there be love and acceptance.

Let there be radiance of joy and transformation on the lips of all who call my name, that I may also experience your peace and joy in Jesus' name. Amen!

Prayer of Confrontation:

In the name of Jesus, I command any evil tree planted over my name to be uprooted right now.

Oh, you stigma attached to my name,

I command you to be separated from me in the name of Jesus.

No more shall my name or personality be identified with evil.

No more shall evil show up when my name is mentioned.

No more shall shame and disgrace appear when my name is called.

The blood of Jesus nullifies the handwriting of ordinances attached to my name.

I declare all evil ordinances null and void in Jesus' name. Amen.

Observations – write your experience after the prayer:

_____
_____
_____

Achievements – what did you gain from this prayer?

_____
_____
_____

CHAPTER ELEVEN

Residence and Address

Residence and Contact Address: On many occasions, when demons are cast out, they usually want to go to the residential home of the victim to re-attack the person at night. Sometimes the demons would even threaten, "We are going to wait for you at home." The demons boast of their ability to return, especially if they are family demons or familiar spirits.

Your contact address may have a loophole for demonic attack. Your address could be a snare to you. Your residence could be a habitation for evil spirits. Where do you live, and what is your environment like? Who are your neighbors, and what kinds of people live with you? What kind of spirituality do they practice?

In order to have legal authority over your home and neighborhood, you would need to clear the spiritual atmosphere surrounding you. Otherwise your prayer and Bible study life will be weakened, and the evil spirits around your neighborhood will torment your life. Once your prayer and Bible Study life is weakened, you are likely to become a powerless Christian.

Also, if a member of your household indulges in diabolical activities such as consulting mysticism and spiritualists for assistance, your home will be invaded by spiritual terrorists, and your Christian life will suffer. Your home and residential address could be an open door to some form of satanic attacks, so it is wise to check through all these avenues and close your doors as fast as you can to avoid infiltration of spiritual terrorists. (See my book on *When Satan went to Church?* and *Solution: Deliverance Ministration to Self and Others* for details on *"Spiritual Doors"*).

Prayer Tactics
(Remember to observe the Spiritual Protocol)

State the Problem:
Need to declare your home illegal for the enemy to dwell therein.

Prayer Focus:
Pray that evil spirits will not co-habit your home.

- That the demons that are evicted outside will not find you nor return to your home.
- That your contact address will be sacred and toxic to the enemy.

- That your residence shall be the habitation of the Holy Spirit even as your body is expected to be the temple of the living God.

The Authority of Scripture: Matthew 12:43-45

The Prayer of Confrontation:
O you demons that claim familiarity with me,
I renounce you in the name of Jesus.
You shall not be my host or guest.
I evict you out of my home in the name of Jesus.

With the authority in the blood of Jesus, you declare that my home shall not be comfortable for your habitation, and my body shall also not be your dwelling place.

In the name of Jesus, I command you to pack your load and go out of my environment, out of my home, out of my life, out of my body, my soul and my spirit.

I shall not see you again, and you shall not come my way.

The blood of Jesus builds a wall between you and me. Amen!!

Observations – write your experience from this prayer:

_____
_____
_____

Achievements – what did you gain from this prayer?

_____
_____
_____

CHAPTER TWELVE

Date and Place of Birth

Date and Place of Birth: What is the story behind your birth and delivery? Find out if there is any omen or confusion around your conception and also the pain and hurts your parents might have been through. This will help you to break any satanic legality around your life. Satan may be claiming legal authority over your life because of the errors committed ignorantly by your parents.

Some people are fond of consulting mediums or spiritualists to inquire about the future of their unborn babies. Consulting some of these oracles could put the child in perpetual bondage or captivity. This will cause the child a lifetime struggle as the oracle consulted would make attempts to possess and control the child's life or destiny.

Prayer Tactics
(Remember to observe the Spiritual Protocol)

State the Problem:
Need to be released from umbilical or conceptual controversy and confusion.

Prayer Focus:
There was a controversy surrounding your conception and birth.

Hence you are bitter or confused.

You are caught up in the web of entanglement that affects your personality and confidence.

You seem to live in a mirage of mess.

You think your situation is hopeless.

The more you try to get out of it

the more pain you feel inside of you.

- You need to renounce your attachment to umbilical curse.
- You need to release yourself from the weakness of your parents.
- You need to disentangle your thoughts form self-condemnation.
- You need to accept the redemption that Christ Jesus gave you on the cross.
- You need to dip yourself in the blood of Jesus and accept the impact of the blood upon your life.
- You need to do a prayer of rededication to assure yourself of having accepted Jesus Christ as your Lord and Savior.

- You need to declare your legal grounds as an heir of the Father through the blood of Jesus Christ.

The Authority of Scripture: Galatians 4:1-7

The Prayer of Confrontation:

Hey, Satan, enough is enough.
You can no longer torment or harass me.
Jesus died to buy my pardon.
By His blood I am made whole.
The Scripture declares that I belong to the Father
And a joint heir with Jesus Christ our Lord.
Therefore, in the name of Jesus, I renounce all manner of contamination
that affects me.
I am saved by the blood, and in the name of Jesus, I shall not
Inherit the sins of my parents.
I declare my freedom in the name of Jesus
I hide myself in the blood of the covenant of the cross of Jesus Christ. Amen!!

Observations – write your experience after the prayer:

_____
_____
_____

Achievements – what did you gain from this prayer?

_____
_____
_____

CHAPTER THIRTEEN

Spiritual Birth

Date and Place of New Birth (Spiritual): After we have been born of the flesh—biologically by our parents, we also need to be born of the spirit—born again. It is very important to be born again because of the sin we inherited from Adam and Eve (John 3:1-7). The process of the new birth regenerates our spirits and relationship with the Almighty God through our Lord and Savior Jesus Christ. To be born again is to be reconnected to God by accepting Jesus Christ as our Lord and Savior.

In order for us to be able to overcome the spiritual interferences we do suffer, we need to make reference to the date we gave our lives to Jesus Christ and became born again. Our spiritual birthday gives us legal authority over Satan and his cohorts. It gives us the evidence that we have confessed Jesus Christ as our Redeemer and Savior, therefore we come under His Lordship for our spiritual authority.

When we recognize and submit to the Lordship of Jesus Christ by referring to our spiritual date of birth, then we are able to overcome the enemy's attack. Our spiritual date of birth is a weapon for declaring our authority to claim legal grounds against interfering spirits.

A demon once exposed a lady who went out of the church to consult a witchdoctor for help. Then she came to church with an intention to share a testimony of "what the Lord has done." As she opened her mouth to share the testimony, the demons began to speak through her, "Why do you want to give credit to another person? The witchdoctor did it. You came to consult us and we assisted you." The lady started manifesting in front of the congregation.

The woman betrayed her salvation and the demons disgraced her. She no longer had a reference point until she rededicated her life to Jesus Christ. She opened up her life to demons by consulting evil spirits for help, and they disgraced her. This is because by leaving the church for the witchdoctor enclave, she allowed the enemy to break into her legal grounds. She opened her doors for the demons to come in, and her life was infested with spiritual pests.

When we sin, we fall short of the glory of God. If we do not confess and repent, after a while we mess up our salvation record. It is necessary and important for us to rededicate our lives in order to straighten up our testimony so that we do not give the enemy any form of authority to invade our lives.

Prayer Tactics
(Remember to observe the Spiritual Protocol)

State the Problem:
You need to close the doors you opened that have allowed the enemy to invade your life.

Prayer Focus:
You have a desperate need, and you also have to make a decision.

Therefore, you need to hear from God.

You have fasted and prayed as much as you can, yet it seems nothing is happening.

Then you decided to take a shortcut to resolve your problem and consulted a clairvoyant or witchdoctor for help. This opened your door, then the enemy came in to plunder you.

- You need to repent from your deed.
- You need to release yourself from the control of a clairvoyant spirit.
- You need to renounce all connections with the clairvoyant/witchdoctor.
- You need to ask the Lord to teach you to be patient and understand the fact that the plans and purposes of God are related to times and seasons.
- You need to re-present your situation to the Lord.
- You need to build up your expectations with the promises of God from the Scriptures.

The Authority of Scripture: Leviticus 17:7

The Prayer:
O Lord and my God, impatience has caused me to stumble into the camp of the enemy.

My weakness has caused me to open my life to the enemy,

And he has taken advantage of me.

I repent of my sins and ask that the blood of Jesus wash and cleanse me.

The Prayer of Confrontation:
Listen, Satan, I shall no longer be deceived.

In the name of Jesus, I command the spirit of impatience to go out of my life.

I shall no longer entertain the spirit of impatience.

I shall no longer consult the witchdoctor and the clairvoyant.

The Scripture declares in Exodus 20 that

There is no other god besides the Most High God,

Therefore, with the authority in the blood of Jesus,

I break any pact I have with the devil.

I shall no longer submit my life to Satan and his cohorts.

I declare the Lordship of Jesus Christ over my life.

This I pray in the name of Jesus Christ my Lord and Redeemer. Amen!

Observations – write your experience after the prayer:

_____
_____
_____

Achievements – what did you gain from this prayer?

_____
_____
_____

CHAPTER FOURTEEN

Religious Affiliation

Church/Fellowship Affiliation: We need to be properly committed to a church or fellowship for covering, feeding, growth and establishment. When we are not committed to a church, we do not receive proper covering, and we are open to the enemy's attack. Many people run away from commitment because they do not want to give tithes and offerings, yet they want the church to be responsible to them. Many people want the Church to be accountable to them, yet they do not understand the importance of tithing and the implication of evading tithing. Many are yet to understand the fact that tithing is the same as taxation. Tithe is paid to God through the church, and taxation is paid to the government through our employers. The consequences of not paying both tithe and taxes are similar.

Well, if you evade tithing, you are a thief, a witch, an adulterer and a robber, and as a result, you are disobedient (Malachi 3). Tithing is a command from God and you must obey it (Deuteronomy 26). If taxation is a law of the land and its evasion is punishable by imprisonment and fines, then tithing must equally be respected and observed. Stop running away from commitment to the Church, and receive proper covering that will protect you from the wiles of the enemy.

When you are not affiliated with any church or fellowship, you are like a homeless person. The devil can get you at anytime. Pride and arrogance can also keep you away from commitment. Self-sufficiency is not a solution for spiritual growth and development. If you do not belong to a church/fellowship, the devil will plunder you, and your family will be open to spiritual interferences. The house of God is your stronghold and God is your Strongman. (See my book on *Pulling Down Satanic Strongholds*).

Prayer Tactics
(Remember to observe the Spiritual Protocol)

State the Problem:
I need to be submissive to authority so that I can be covered.

Prayer Focus:
I pray that the Lord will teach me to be humble and submissive to authority.

- That I may stay committed to other ministries

- That I may know and understand the importance of loyalty
- So that I can receive divine covering at the appropriate place
- That the Lord will direct me to a place where I will be able to receive and serve so that I can be fulfilled

The Authority of Scripture:
Do not forsake the assembly of the brethren (Hebrews 10:24-25).

The Prayer:
Lord Jesus, thank You for giving me the opportunity to understand the importance of covering and commitment in my Christian life.

Lord, teach me to fellowship with others,

As Your Word encourages us not to forsake the assembly of the brethren

Lord, I ask that You will direct me to a fellowship that You have prepared for me.

Teach me to be humble and committed so that I can serve with loyalty.

Teach me to submit myself to correction

That I may not falter nor fall away from the truth

Thank you, Lord, because You have heard my prayer.

This I pray in Jesus' name. Amen.

Observations – write your experience after the prayer:

_____
_____
_____

Achievements – what did you gain from this prayer?

_____
_____
_____

CHAPTER FIFTEEN

Marital Status

Marriage is one of the greatest and earliest institutions that God created when He made a home for the first family in the Garden of Eden (Genesis 2). The manner we approach marriage is a great concern to God. The legal authority on marriage is a threat to the kingdom of Satan. That is why the home is a target for satanic attacks—harassment and terrorism.

The manner in which we approach marriage— how and whom we marry usually create a lot of confusion in the spiritual realm. Therefore, we need to be conscious not to open doors of curses upon our marriages even before we step into them. When the spiritual protocol that guides marriage is broken, then the devil takes advantage and begins to attack the home. Even innocent children are affected in the war that will later emerge in the family.

Some of the spiritual warfare that we suffer are the result of the mistakes our parents made ignorantly. The errors were made when they stepped into marriage without observing certain spiritual protocols that are Biblically institutionalized. Every family has a tradition that they expect one to observe when it comes to marriage.

Some of the traditions are Scriptural while some are ungodly and also have some demonic implications. Christians around the world have begun to oppose or ignore ungodly approaches to marriage. However, as much as we try to avoid some of the traditions that are not suitable for our Christian beliefs, we should also endeavor to establish our legal grounds to avoid demonic interferences as a result of curses and anger that might be released into our marriages.

However, we must also bear in mind that we cannot establish successful legal grounds if we do not submit to Biblical truths and walk in the fear of God. Our personal weaknesses can cause a greater havoc that will open the door for Satan and his cohorts to torment the marriage later. There are many marriages that are suffering from curses and anger from family members and friends.

It is wise to make peace with the individuals who are upset in order for one to be secured. Otherwise, the relationship concerned would continue to suffer unprecedented attacks either now or in the future, and innocent children born to such families will suffer the repercussion of the errors made by the parents.

Prayer Tactics
(Remember to observe the Spiritual Protocol)

State the Problem:
My marriage is under constant attack. It is as though somebody is not happy with my marriage.

Prayer Focus:
Pray that God will reveal the cause of the attack.

- That God will help us to forgive those who have cursed our relationship.
- We need to break the negative pronouncement that is affecting our home.
- We need to seal all the loopholes that use give the enemy an opportunity to interfere with our home.

The Authority of Scripture:
What God has joined together, let no man put asunder (Genesis 2:23-24; Matthew 19:6).

The Prayer:
Father in heaven, I thank You for Your love and care for our family. Thank You for being the Lord of our lives.

Father, we also thank You for exposing the works of the enemy that are interfering with our home.

Your word declares that no one should put asunder what God has joined together.

Therefore, in the name of Jesus, we rebuke the devourer that has been attacking this home.

In the name of Jesus, we renounce any negative pronouncement that has been made over this home.

In the name of Jesus, we erase the handwriting of ordinances meant against us.

We release our home from the pangs of the enemy,

In the name of Jesus, we set our home free from the forces of darkness.

We ask the blood of Jesus to wash and cleanse our home from all manner of contamination.

We seal our marriage with the blood of Jesus.

In the name of Jesus Christ Our Lord and Savior, we pray that the enemy will no longer have access to our home. Amen!

Observations – write your experience after the prayer:

_____
_____
_____

Achievements – what did you gain from this prayer?

_____
_____
_____

CHAPTER SIXTEEN

Children and Siblings

Biological and adopted children and siblings (including step-brothers and sisters): When you are going through deliverance ministration, do not leave your children and siblings out. Make sure they are represented in your presentation. Sometimes the trouble with one person is a problem with the whole family. I have observed cases where a spirit left a person who was receiving ministration and bounced into another member of the family. Thus whatever is wrong with one person affects the whole family. Therefore, it is important to bring all members of the family under God's protection.

Prayer Tactics
(Remember to observe the Spiritual Protocol)

State the Problem:
My children seem to be going through the same cycle of problems that I have suffered.

Prayer Focus:
That my children will not inherit the difficulties that I have encountered in my life

- That my children will not pay for the sins of my fathers and mothers
- That the Lord will block the transmission of curses that has been flowing in our family from past generations
- That my children will not be disobedient
- That the members of my family and siblings will not be wayward

The Authority of Scripture:
"The fathers have eaten sour grapes, and the children's teeth are set on edge?" (Ezekiel 18:2)

The Prayer:
O Lord our God and Maker,
We appreciate the work of Your hands,
For You are the great God of wonders.
We thank You for Jesus Christ and the blood that was shed at Calvary.
We thank You for dying to redeem us and to buy our pardon.

Because of Your blood we rebuke the flow of evil from our family.

With the authority in the blood of Jesus,

We uproot the tree of curses bearing fruit of evil in our children.

We command the tree of curses to be uprooted from our family in the name of Jesus

We command the destruction of the tree of evil

In the name of Jesus, we declare that it shall no longer exist in our family in the name of Jesus.

In the name of Jesus Christ Our Lord and Savior, we release our children from suffering the consequences of the curses that have affected our family in the name of Jesus Christ Our Lord and Savior. Amen!

Observations – write your experience after the prayer:

_____
_____
_____

Achievements – what did you gain from this prayer?

_____
_____
_____

CHAPTER SEVENTEEN

Country of Origin

Country of Origin (From where your parents migrated or claim of originality): Our country of origin may be a snare to us because of problems and atrocities committed by relations and other nationals. If the people of our origin do practice occultism and mysticism, it is likely that curses might have been invoked that trigger disaster and suffering.

In view of such disturbances, we need to break the curses and also renounce our association with the spiritual entities that control that nation's territory. Otherwise we will suffer evil interferences from generational and territorial demons and curses.

Prayer Tactics
(Remember to observe the Spiritual Protocol)

State the Problem:
I need a release from the territorial spirits that control my life because of my native origin.

Prayer Focus:
That I will be free from the territorial spirits that control members of my family

- That I may release myself from all manner of superstitious beliefs that have entangled my life because of my native origin
- That my siblings and children will no longer be controlled and contaminated by the evil forces that rule over the city where we dwell

The Authority of Scripture:
Deuteronomy 7

The Prayer:
Great is Jehovah God, who has created all things.
Greater is He who knows all that concerns me.
May His name be exalted in my life.
Because Jesus Christ is Lord over my life, in the name of Jesus
I reject the control of any other spirit or power
That attempts to influence my life.
In the name of Jesus, I reject any form of territorial control over my body, soul and spirit.

Listen to me, you powers and principalities of darkness that control this city, in the name of Jesus, you shall have no control over me.

In the name of Jesus, you shall not influence my life.

Jesus Christ is Lord over my life, and my allegiance is unto Him

Therefore, I am no longer under your satanic domain.

I am protected and sealed by the blood that Jesus shed for me.

I command you, Satan, to be gone out of my life and environment right now in the name of Jesus.

I shall not see you again and you shall not visit me nor come by me.

The blood of Jesus builds a wall of protection around me

To cover and deliver me from your interferences.

This I declare and pray in the name of Jesus Christ. Amen.

Observations – write your experience after the prayer:

_____
_____
_____

Achievements – what did you gain from this prayer?

_____
_____
_____

CHAPTER EIGHTEEN

Religious belief and Idolatry

Family and Historical Background: Ancestral Worship, Family Worship, Regional Worship, National Worship: The religious practices of a family and the community they belong to have an impact on their spiritual lives and belief system. Some people claim to be born again, yet they are holding on to certain beliefs that have become a stumbling block to their progressiveness. The belief they hold on to is a hindrance to their achievements. Set goals are facing stiff oppositions because our belief system is a demonic stronghold in our lives.

Some of the belief systems and principles we hold on to are not only demonic but are also self-bewitchment. Sometimes we bewitch ourselves with principles that God has not given to us, meanwhile we find it difficult to keep the Ten Commandments faithfully. Certain principles and beliefs are appropriate for certain times and seasons but not for our general life endeavors. We need to be delivered from self-witchcraft.

Having been born again, the old things must be allowed to pass away so that new things can come. As long as we hold on to our ancestral beliefs and background, we are not able to make progress in the Christian faith and in the spiritual realm. This is because our identity in the spiritual realm is still the same. We need to make effective changes in our lifestyle in order to disentangle ourselves from ancestral beliefs.

Until we move out of the old house, we cannot enjoy the new home in Christendom. Our spiritual identity is very important. We need to know the kind of spiritual identity that we have in order to overcome ancestral spirits.

Idolatry - Spiritualism and Mysticism (Witchcraft, Idolatry, Occult, Psychic, Palmistry, Crystalism, Fortune-telling, Magic, Medium, Ouija Board, Voodoo, Herbalism, Others): Have you ever been involved with or consulted any of these practitioners? What are your reasons and what did you achieve?

Involvement in mysticism and spirituality is described in the Bible as idolatry. Involvement could be at any level and by any means. You could have been involved directly or indirectly, directly by being a practitioner and indirectly by contributing to its practices. No matter how you got involved, whether by force, by persuasion or by parental upbringing, you are marked by an identity that gives Satan and his cohorts the legal authority to interfere with your family and yourself. Unless you break your spiritual connection with your past involvement, the negative identity will linger on.

Consultation has to do with employing the services of the practitioners of spiritual mysticism. Many people seek their services because they believe in the power of occultism. Your intention for consulting any of these mediums could be for positive or negative reasons, but it does not change the Word of God. Whatever you achieved for consulting a spiritualist has some form of repercussion. One of the repercussions is the fact that you will be marked for demonic control; therefore, you will suffer evil interferences directly or indirectly at one point in your life. You may not notice the interferences until you have forgotten the cause or source of it. Unfortunately, you may turn around and accuse another person of bewitching your life. You will have forgotten that past indulgence has led to witch-hunting, (See my book on *Receive and Maintain Your Deliverance on Legal Grounds* and *Pulling Down Satanic Strongholds* for details).

Prayer Tactics
(Remember to observe the Spiritual Protocol)

State the Problem:
Need to renounce past indulgence in mysticism and superstitious beliefs

Prayer Focus:
That I will no longer subscribe to superstitious beliefs

- That my family will no longer indulge in mysticism and spiritism
- That my family will fear the Lord and walk in His ways
- That we will no longer bewitch ourselves through superstitions and diabolic indulgence

The Authority of Scripture:
"Thou shall worship no other God besides me" (Exodus 20:3).

The Prayer:
Great God of Wonders, we adore You and exalt Your holy name. You are great and there is none like You.

Lord, I ask for forgiveness on behalf of my family and myself.

We have unknowingly indulged in mysticism and spiritism.

We have depended on superstitions and gone against Your will.

Today, we acknowledge our weaknesses and indulgence in idolatry.

We repent from our sins and plead the blood of Jesus to wash and cleanse us from our filthiness.

The Confrontation:
In the name of Jesus, I rebuke the spirit of deception that influences my family.

In the name of Jesus, I renounce any ties with mysticism and spiritism.

In the name of Jesus, I release myself from any covenant that was made knowingly and unknowingly to attract religious spirits into my family.

Scripture declares that I shall not worship any other god besides Jehovah God, therefore, in the name of Jesus Christ, I sever any relationship with demonic gods.

In the name of Jesus, I declare my freedom in the spiritual realm and in the physical realm.

Observations – write your experience after the prayer:

_____
_____
_____

Achievements – what did you gain from this prayer?

_____
_____
_____

CHAPTER NINETEEN

Family Background

Family and Relationship Traits (Father's side traits, Mother's side traits, Personal traits, Marital traits): What are the frequent problems that confront members of your family and create unforeseen or notable obstacles, such as **Disasters, Poverty, Deaths, Accidents, Miscarriages, Insanity, Sicknesses, Failures, Disappointments, Divorce and Separation?** How do some of these problems affect you?

There are separate issues emanating from your father's side and your mother's side because both are from different family backgrounds. If you are married, then you have four different families to deal with as regards both sides of your spouse families. Then your spouse and you will also be treated on a separate note because your personal problems may be different from that of your spouse.

The problems that are frequent occurrences among family members are classified as physical inheritances, and they need to be dealt with and uprooted because they run through the family like a tree that bears fruits in its season. Such problems also turn out to become family curse. (See my book, *Receive and Maintain Your Deliverance on Legal Grounds*)

Prayer Tactics
(Remember to observe the Spiritual Protocol)

State the Problem:
I am going through the same difficulties that my parents went through. My siblings are wayward and my children seem to be displaying the same traits.

Prayer Focus:
That I will not inherit the curses and weaknesses of my parents

- That my children will not inherit our weaknesses
- That the blessing of salvation through Jesus Christ will be manifested in my children
- That the blood of Jesus will flow through my children
- That the fear of God will arrest every member of my family

The Authority of Scripture:
"Believe on the Lord Jesus Christ, and you will be saved, you and your household" (Acts 16:31).

The Prayer of Confrontation:

In the name of Jesus, I come against all manner of evil properties that I inherited from my families.

I renounce the transfer of evil from my parents to my family and myself.

In the name of Jesus, I break the link that permits the flow of character inheritance that is evil.

I declare that the salvation of my life shall affect my household

I declare that everyone in my household shall be convicted of sin

And they all be shall be saved according to the Word of the Lord.

I declare that demons shall no longer rule over my household.

I declare that members of my family shall no longer subscribe to satanic entities.

I declare that my household shall come under divine arrest in the name of Jesus Christ our Lord and Savior. Amen!

Observations – write your experience after the prayer:

_____
_____
_____

Achievements – what did you gain from this prayer?

_____
_____
_____

CHAPTER TWENTY

Character Inheritance

—∞—

Character Traits (Anger, Pride, Impatience, Malice, Strive, Fornication/Adultery/Sexual Misbehavior, Uncleanness, Idolatry/Sorcery, Hatred, Envy, Jealousy, Selfish ambitions, Contentions, Dissensions, Drunkenness, Heresies): Which of these character traits are common in your spouse, family members and your personal life (Galatians 5: 16-21)?

More often than not, we have been betrayed by our characters especially where we have lacked self-control and misbehaved before dignitaries or individuals who hold us in high esteem. Many individuals have lost quality relationships and high paying or executive jobs because of lack of character control. Our character is the greatest image we have to portray to the world. Even where the work of our hands has exceeded our characters, the excellence of our behavior has either lifted us up or our weakness has betrayed us and thrown some of us into the pit of shame and disgrace.

After reading my book, *Anger: Get Rid of It*, a young man who lost an employment because of anger, and was heading towards destruction of his destiny because of lack of self-control, shared this testimony:

> I decided not to get angry with anybody again in my life. I have lost good opportunities in life because of anger. I once vented my anger against a man who had recommended me for one of the best positions on my job. The man was good, he ignored me. But the director wanted to drop me, so he invited me to his office and said, "I would have called off both your employment and recommendation today, but the very man you disrespected has always acted as your angel. Go and dump your foolishness in the thrash and change your character." I was confused to learn that the very man I tried to destroy in my anger had been saving me from trouble.
>
> From that day, I decided never to seek for help, then the same man got hold of your book and gave it to me. While reading the book, I decided never to express my dissatisfaction through anger again, no matter what the situation may be. I'm still on that job enjoying the best of employment benefits.

Everyone needs to be involved in character development program for family and self in order to overcome the ordeal that the works of the flesh bring to us directly or indirectly. Our characters are like a tree bearing fruits that and reflected in our behavior and attitudes as we go through our daily endeavors. The branches of the tree could be flourishing and attractive to the censure of all eyes; they could also be hidden from the glare of the public. If the tree is good, then the branches and the fruits will be good. But if the tree is evil, the branches and the fruits cannot be good.

Our relations and family members are part of the branches and fruits that came out of our lives. If we do not adhere to self-control, wherever we stand, the negative fruits from our children and other family members could pose as hindrances to the beautiful garden we spend our whole life to nurture.

Deliverance ministration helps us to uproot briers and tares from our garden. Some of the tares are just like the wheat we have spent all our lives sowing, and others may have developed thorns that choke and hinder the growth of our wheat. Whatever the situation is, God has given us a weapon for solution, and we need to apply it effectively. That is what this book seeks to do for you. The lessons are yours for the asking. Uproot that character and enjoy your salvation in Christ Jesus. Amen!

Prayer Tactics
(Remember to observe the Spiritual Protocol)

State the Problem:
I need to control my character traits.

Prayer Focus:
That my character will no longer be a hindrance to my faith and destiny

- That I will be conscious of Jesus Christ as my Lord and Savior
- That I will be an example to the world around me
- That my character will reflect the image and likeness of the living God

The Authority of Scripture: Genesis 1:26.

The Prayer:
Father in heaven, there is none like You.
You are great and Your mercies endure forever.
Thank You for reminding me to return to Your image.

The Prayer of Confrontation:
The Scripture declares that I am created in the image of God,
Therefore, I renounce any ungodly image in my body, spirit and soul.

In the name of Jesus, I command any evil tree bearing fruits of unrighteousness to be uprooted out of my life right now.

You spirit of anger, you will no longer control or influence my attitude.

With the authority in the name of Jesus, I command you to be uprooted out of my life.

The blood of Jesus releases me from the stronghold of anger.

Observations – write your experience after the prayer:

_____
_____
_____

Achievements – what did you gain from this prayer?

_____
_____
_____

CHAPTER TWENTY-ONE

Emotional Inheritance

Hurts and Pains (Frustration, Suppression, Oppression, Depression, Rejection, Fear, Attacks, Prayerlessness, Lack of Bible Study): According to Scripture, it is human for anyone to experience hurt and pain, but it is not normal to hold the offense against the victims, therefore we are required to forgive and forget. The Lord's Prayer teaches us to forgive so that we can also receive pardon from the Most High God.

For us to receive complete deliverance, we need to examine the cause of our hurts and pains and deal with them. If we avoid the root cause of our problems, we would not be able to release ourselves from pain. Recently I was ministering to a lady who claimed she has suffered frequent hurts from other people, so she decided to seclude herself in order to avoid further hurts. When she separated herself, the enemy filled her mind with false accusations and suspicion as well as insecurity.

Although I did not know the details of her story, I felt she needed to make restitution in order to be free. After the ministration, I encouraged her to make peace with her suspected offenders. While she was still initiating the peace, the spirit of joy came upon her, and she began to laugh. Then she said, "I feel something is gone out of me, and I feel lighter and relieved." That is the power of forgiveness. Jesus said, "My peace I leave with you." Therefore, any situation that interferes with your peace are not of God. Making restitution with the individuals who offend you will bring you into restoration of fellowship with the Holy Spirit.

Prayer Tactics
(Remember to observe the <u>Spiritual Protocol</u>)

State the Problem:
I need to learn to sow love so that I can receive love against hurts and pains.

Prayer Focus:
That I may understand the love of God

- That I will sow love into others lives
- That I will open up to love so that I can receive same
- That I will no longer seclude myself out of suspicion
- That I will no longer give room to hurts and pains

- That I will no longer allow the enemy to rob me of the joy of salvation

The Authority of Scripture:
"Peace I leave with you, My peace I give to you . . . (John 14:27).

The Prayer:
Dear Lord, thank You for the promise of peace and love.
Thank You that Your peace gives me security,
And Your love gives me love protection.
Lord, I ask that You will enable me to believe that
Your love and peace is sufficient for me
So that I will not feel insecure and rejected among the brethren.
Help me to accept other with love and understanding.
Help me to hold on to Your trust instead of human beings.
Help to mature so that I will not be hurt by the weaknesses of others.
Teach me to sow love and to depend on You for my blessings.
This I pray in the name of Jesus Christ. Amen!

Confrontation:
I come against the works of the flesh in the name of Jesus Christ my Savior.
I come against the spirit of hurts and disappointments.

You shall no longer control my emotions.

I cast you out of my heart, out of my spirit, out of my behavior and out of my attitude.

You will no longer control nor manipulate my life,

And I shall no longer be a host to the works of the flesh.

Go out of my environment right now.

The blood of Jesus is against you.

The blood of Jesus washes and cleanses every aspect of my emotions.

The blood of Jesus releases me from the works of the flesh.

The blood of Jesus sets me from hurts and disappointment.

I release the peace and love of God to reign in my life.

I release my heart and soul to receive and accept the love of God

In the name of Jesus Christ I pray. Amen!

Observations – write your experience after the prayer:

_____
_____
_____

Achievements – what did you gain from this prayer?

_____
_____
_____

CHAPTER TWENTY-TWO

Material and Financial Inheritances

Challenges (**Employment situation, Financial situation, Relationship situation**): People face challenges in their lifetime everywhere, but some situations are quite abnormal and sometimes beyond our comprehension. We are tempted to ask questions like "What have I done? Why me?" Yet, we get no answer. The fact is that we might have broken a rule somewhere and one day we will be required to pay a price for it.

It could also be that the fathers have eaten the sour grapes and the teeth of the children are set on edge. Therefore, the children are forced to pay for the sins committed by the fathers. It may also be that an unfortunate child has inherited curses that are flowing down from 200 years of sin and its repercussions.

Whatever the problems are, God has provided us with solutions in the Word through deliverance ministration. The Lord is our refuge and deliverer.

Prayer Tactics
(Remember to observe the Spiritual Protocol).

State the Problem:
Need solutions to the challenges in my life.

Prayer Focus:
To distinguish myself from the faults of my parents and forefathers

- That my generation will not pay the price for the faults of the past generations
- That there shall no longer be a false inheritance in my family
- That the past will not control my present life

The Authority of Scripture:
"... **With God all things are possible (Matthew 19:26).**"

The Prayer:
Dear Lord, I thank You for Your love and care for me.

Thank You for revealing Your truth to me.

Thank You for revealing the secrets of my family to me

So that I will disentangle myself from the sins of the foreparents

Prayer of Confrontation
Satan, listen to me;
you cannot charge me with the sins of my forefathers and mothers.
You cannot hold me in captivity for the sins I did not commit.
Jesus died to set me free.
The blood of Jesus has paid the price of every debt I owe directly or indirectly.
Since I have accepted Jesus Christ as my Lord and Savior,
I do not owe you anything, because the death of Jesus has erased my debt.
I have been bought over by shedding of His blood and the price He paid,
Therefore, you cannot hold me down in captivity.
I declare my liberty in the name of Jesus Christ.
With the authority in the blood of Jesus, I command every chain in my life to be broken.
I release myself from every satanic imprisonment.
I am free in the name of Jesus Christ my Lord and Savior. Amen

Observations – write your experience after the prayer:

_____
_____
_____

Achievements – what did you gain from this prayer?

_____
_____
_____

CHAPTER TWENTY-THREE

Burdens and Concerns

Burdens and Concerns (spiritual problems, physical problems, emotional problems): There are people who carry other persons' burden by expressing concern for everything that they hear or see. In the process, they suffer hurts and disappointments because they feel no one cares as much as they do. If God calls you into the ministry of helps, then you will not have to carry the burden by yourself. You will only do what the Lord sends you to do. If you carry a burden that the Lord did not put on you, you will be pregnant with false conception that will later bruise your efforts.

Carrying burdens and concerns includes fighting wars that are attached to them. It is like an intruding attitude. Unless individuals give you permission to carry their burdens, do not get involved, otherwise you will be betrayed to the enemy or left alone in the middle of the battle. Do not engage in a war that God has not given you authority to fight. If God assigns you to a war, he will also equip you for battle. It is dangerous to engage in any war without adequate preparation. It is dangerous because you will be wounded very badly.

Difference between a burden and a concern

Concern is an expression of worry and anxiety: Although Christians are expected to show concern for others, as in the case of the "Good Samaritan," we are not to bruise ourselves with worry and anxiety. Scripture warns us to be anxious for nothing, but to cast our cares upon the Lord. Worry and anxiety does not solve any problem, but rather cause sicknesses like hypertension and headaches. The birds of the air and the lilies of the valley do not worry about their sustenance. Why then should humans worry about their survival?

Some problems are spiritual, and some are physical while others are emotional. Some parents seek the attention of clairvoyant for everything. They suspect other people for every problem that besieges them. Some mothers are always worried as though they have the power to change the situation that their wards encounter, even if it is their fault. They worry about everything, yet some of these mothers have ignored the foundational responsibilities of bringing up their children in the fear of the Lord. They have refused to teach their children to walk in the fear of the Lord, hence the children do not know the essence of accepting correction nor lending to teachable spirits. Some parents overprotect their children and prevent them from experiencing the realities of life.

The consequences of such an upbringing are the exhibition of worry and anxiety. Beloved, turn over your concerns to Jesus, and everything will be alright.

Also there are individuals who are proud and arrogant. This category of people will neither take instruction nor direction from anybody. As much as they go to church and are actively involved, they have no fear of God. They will always do whatever they set their hearts on instead of taking advice from mature or experienced persons. They will cause trouble for everyone and create situations that call for public concerns. Whatever the situation is, do not allow the concern you have for other persons to become a burden that you cannot handle. Remember that prayer is the "master key."

Burden is carrying a heavy load or experiencing a situation that is difficult to bear. There are people who are highly ambitious. As a result, they carry burdens that the Lord has already taken care of. We are to cast our burdens upon the Lord and He will bear it all. A burden is like a yoke around a person's neck. It is heavy and suppressing. It keeps a person below and never on top, beneath and never above.

When God gives a burden, it is usually for prayer and intercession. We are therefore called to stand in the gap and pray, but we are not to bear the burden as if it is our responsibility to solve it. Just take it to the Lord in prayer, and the Holy Spirit will turn the situation around. Amen.

Prayer Tactics
(Remember to observe the Spiritual Protocol)

State the Problem:
Need deliverance from carrying false burdens and concerns.

Prayer Focus:
That I will no longer be disappointed if my work is not appreciated

- That I will do just what the Lord sends me to do
- That I will not try to be what I am not
- That I will no longer pick up burdens I do not understand
- That I will not impose myself on people to help them

The Authority of Scripture:
"Be anxious for nothing . . ." (Philippians 4:6).

The Prayer:
Great God of Wonders,
The Almighty and Everlasting Father,
The King of Glory,
The knower of all things,
You are the God of wisdom and understanding.
You are the God of knowledge and judgment.
You are the God of mercy and grace.
You are the God of solution.
This day, I realize my weakness,

So I ask for pardon and correction,
That I will no longer take upon myself
The burdens that You have not assigned to me.
Teach me to be sensitive to Your instructions.
Teach me to follow Your directions.
Grant me thy wisdom,
That I may not fail.
This I pray in the name of Jesus Christ our Savior. Amen!

Observations – write your experience after the prayer:

_____
_____
_____

Achievements – what did you gain from this prayer?

_____
_____
_____

CHAPTER TWENTY-FOUR

The Deliverance War

Deliverance Prayer is warfare. It is a confrontation with the enemy. It is not a plea or a cry but war against the enemy. The approach towards deliverance prayer must be aggressive and with desperation. Any one intending to go into deliverance ministration must be ready to be a warrior. One must be ready to go to the battlefield and fight with strategies that would beat the enemy hands down.

Anytime you decide to minister deliverance to an individual or yourself, you are initiating a war against the enemy. Therefore, getting into deliverance ministration means you are up to the battlefront to release that person from the camp of the enemy.

Equipment for Battle

Do not go to battle unequipped. You must make sure that you are well equipped and ready for battle. Do not initiate wars you cannot fight. Do not open doors you cannot close. Do not open too many doors at a time. Take one step at a time and be cautious of what you intend to do. Map out your strategies properly so that the enemy will not take advantage of you and weary you out of the battle.

As a warrior, you need the Word of God, which is the major sword of the Spirit for all battles. The Word of God is the shield and buckler, the helmet of salvation strong enough to pull down satanic strongholds and destroy the wiles of the enemy. In order for the Word to be effective in your mouth, you need to observe the various instructions discussed in this book. (See the other tittles listed for more instructions, *When Satan Went to Church* and *Pulling Down Satanic Strongholds*)

Prayer Tactics
(Remember to observe the Spiritual Protocol)

State the Problem:
I need to be equipped for war

Prayer Focus:
That the Lord will grant me wisdom and understanding to manage the wars that confront me

- I need wisdom to discern the times and season for war.
- I need wisdom to understand the pattern of warfare.
- I need instruction to handle the weapons of war.

The Authority of Scripture:
Teach my hands to make war (Psalm 18:34).

The Prayer:
The Lord is good and He is worthy to be praised.

Lord, I ask that You will open my eyes of understanding to discern types of wars and how to confront the enemy.

Lord, I ask that You will grant me wisdom
to understand the tactics of the enemy.

Lord, I ask that You will teach me strategies of war, that I will be bold to confront the enemy, that I will stand like a soldier,

And fight with confidence that You have already given me the victory. Amen!

Observations – write your experience after the prayer:

_____
_____
_____

Achievements – what did you gain from this prayer?

_____
_____
_____

CHAPTER TWENTY-FIVE

Prisoners of War

So many people are prisoners of war in Satan's camp. Some people initiated wars that they could not handle while some went to war without being adequately equipped. Hence they were wounded or captured by the enemy. Such individuals need to be released by warring against the enemy but not by pleading with Satan. Satan has never been merciful, so he cannot pardon anybody.

In order to release such individuals from satanic imprisonment, Satan must be confronted with aggression. You must confront Satan with your spiritual weapons and with boldness. You must confront him with your spiritual connection and allegiance to the Lord Jesus Christ. You must confront him with your spiritual integrity as a born-again Christian. You must confront him with the intention to win and set the captive free.

When you get to the prison gate, you need to eliminate the prison guards or threaten them to flight.

Then go on to pull down the prison gate. In order to release the prisoner of war, you have to break the chains on their hands and feet before you take them out of the prison.

- You must command the prison gates to open.
- You must command the chains of imprisonment to be broken.
- You must declare the Lordship of Jesus Christ over the individual's life.
- You must proclaim the individual free in the name of Jesus.
- You must build a hedge of protection around the individual to avoid re-attack and re-arrest.
- You must seal the individual with the blood of Jesus Christ to repel the enemy from harassing that person.

Prayer Tactics
(Remember to observe the Spiritual Protocol)

State the Problem:
I need release from satanic imprisonment.

Prayer Focus:
I need to break the chains of captivity from my life.

- That I will no longer live under satanic control
- That the work of the flesh will no longer manifest in my life
- That the fruits of the Spirit will reflect in my behavior and attitude
- That my mind will be saturated with the Word of God
- That my language will reflect the presence of God in my life

The Authority of Scripture: Isaiah 61:1-2

The Prayer:
The Lord is great and He is worthy of our praise.
Great is Jehovah God the creator of my life.
You are the Alpha and Omega, the Beginning and the End.
There is none like You throughout eternity.
Thank You for life and thank You for restoration.
Thank You for giving me the opportunity to have life and to know You more and more.

Prayer of Confrontation:
Because of the blood of Jesus Christ and the Name that is above all other names,
Satan can no longer hold me bound.
In the name of Jesus,
I command my release from all manner of imprisonment.
In the name of Jesus,

I command the chains in my life to be broken right now.

In the name of Jesus,

I command the prison gates to open.

In the name of Jesus,

I render every satanic cohort powerless.

In the name of Jesus,

Satan, your powers are broken, open the prison gates.

Your powers are broken; let me out.

Your powers are broken; you shall no longer control my life.

The blood of Jesus is against you.

I declare my freedom in the name of Jesus Christ.

I declare my liberty in the name of Jesus Christ.

In the name of Jesus Christ, I'm no longer a prisoner of war.

The blood of Jesus Christ builds a hedge of protection around me.

I am covered by the blood of Jesus Christ.

Thank you, Lord, for setting me free from satanic imprisonment. Amen!

Observations – write your experience after the prayer:

_____

_____

_____

Achievements – what did you gain from this prayer?

_____
_____
_____

CHAPTER TWENTY-SIX

Deliverance Prayer

This chapter gives you specific instructions on how to engage in deliverance prayer. In order to achieve results from deliverance prayer, you must tithe your time and be ready to achieve a goal. Set aside a time that you will be investing into this prayer. You may set aside a month or more to do this warfare consistently until your battle is won. One day is not enough for this type of deliverance prayer. Deliverance prayer is warfare and can last for up to three months or one year, depending on your consistency and aggressiveness. If you are desperate, then you need to fight the war in your life with aggression. A desperate fighter fights vigorously, and a wounded lion fights with aggression.

Instruction for Deliverance Prayer:
1. The usual time for a warfare prayer is between 12:00 midnight and 5:00 a.m. or between

11:30 a.m.–2:30p.m. Choose a time that is convenient for you and stick to it.
2. This is a prayer of deliverance, so you need to speak out to your own hearing because you are addressing the spirits that are interfering with your life or obstructing you in some way.
3. Deliverance prayer is warfare, so you need to walk around the house and speak the word to the hearing of everything in your home—including your bedroom, bathroom and kitchen so that everything in your environment will hear the Word of the Lord. Then the strange spirits that have turned your house into some type of prison will go away because the Word of God is power.
4. If you do the prayer as instructed, you will experience some reactions in your body. There is power in the Word of God. The strange spirit troubling you will begin to react through vomiting, spiting, itching, sweating, dizziness, drowsiness, stomach discomfort and similar things. Do not call the medical doctor, but continue to do the prayer until that reaction stops. These reactions are signs that the interfering spirits are exiting from your body or home; therefore do not stop the prayer until you are completely delivered.
5. Write all the things that are troubling you on a sheet of notebook page before you start the prayer. It is important to list out the problems

otherwise you will forget; and you will not be able to achieve the purpose of this prayer.

The Prayer:

1. Read a chapter from the gospel of John each day.
2. Use each verse of the Scripture to eliminate negative things from your life and also to confess good things into your life as indicated by each verse of Scripture.
3. Reading the book of John as though you are praying is very important, so read it loud to your hearing as instructed above.
4. When you have finished with the book of John, go on to Psalm 18.
5. Read Psalm 18 aloud to your hearing.
6. Use each verse of Psalm 18 to release yourself from each of the problems that is confronting you as listed in your notebook.
7. Use each verse like soap and a sponge to renounce every problem in your life.
8. Making reference to Scripture, use the blood of Jesus to erase the plan of the enemy that is meant against you.
9. Please use Scriptures to fight every battle in your life, and your life will never be the same again.
10. If you do this prayer as instructed, you will have a unique deliverance experience, and the devil will no longer interfere with you.

Weapons for Rebuking the Devourer

1. Declare the fact that you pay your tithe and have never failed in your duty to do so.
2. Declare the fact that you contribute to the welfare of the ministry you belong to and have been faithful in supporting the Kingdom of God.
3. Declare the fact that you are faithful in your commitment in fellowship, and you are a child of God.
4. Declare the promises that the Lord has spoken concerning those who are faithful in paying their tithe.
5. Hold on to the promises concerning those who are faithful in fulfilling their responsibilities in the house of the Lord.
6. Declare the promises of God to protect your source of income and your vineyard.
7. Declare His promises to prevent the evil one from sowing seeds of discord into your vineyard because of your salvation in Jesus Christ and your tithing.
8. Declare His promises concerning you as an individual.
9. Remember to confess your faults and weaknesses so that the enemy will not hold anything against you.
10. Remember that you can only be confident in your declaration after you have covered yourself with the blood of Jesus.

11. Remember that your confession will help your declaration to be effective.
12. Having made the various declarations, begin to declare the Word of God to rebuke the devourer to take his hands off your wealth and prosperity.
13. Take the letter that contains the evil report and begin to renounce and rebuke the contents that are meant against you.
14. Begin to declare confusion in the camp of the enemy so that whatever devilish plans are made against you will not prosper.
15. Assuming you have a court case, begin to ask God for favor to go before the law court so that you can gain favor of the law.
16. Begin to put the word of the Lord in the mouth of the judge so that the counsel of the Most High God will be fulfilled on the day of the judgment.
17. Assuming you have employment, business or financial discord, begin to declare your prosperity as a child of God and pull down every satanic enterprise meant to frustrate your source of income.
18. Reverse the Curse
Reverse curses directed to you, and replace them with blessings.

Prayer Tactics
(Remember to observe the <u>Spiritual Protocol</u>)

State the Problem:

_____
_____
_____

Prayer Focus:

_____
_____
_____

The Authority of Scripture:

_____
_____
_____

The Prayer:

_____
_____
_____

The Prayer of Confrontation:

_____
_____
_____

Reverse the curse:

_____
_____
_____

Plant the Blessings:

_____
_____
_____

Observations – write your experience after the prayer:

_____
_____
_____

Achievements – what did you gain from this prayer?

_____
_____
_____

CHAPTER TWENTY-SEVEN

Prayer of Confrontation

Walk around the room,
It is a war of confrontation.
Show aggression,
And terrorize the enemy.
Dethrone the devil,
And subdue him.
You are a warrior,
A soldier of the cross
Be bold, and be strong,
Be steadfast and be unmoveable
For the Lord is with you. Amen!

Confronting the Enemy with Psalm 18

The Word- Approach God with an expression of love and from romantic perspective:

1. I will love You, O LORD, my strength.

The Prayer:
Jesus, I love You. I know Thou art mine. You died on the cross to save me. Thank You for love and care over my life. Your love for me is greater than my mind could ever comprehend. Praise be unto You. Amen!

Prayer Tactics
(Remember to observe the <u>Spiritual Protocol</u>)

State the Problem:
You want to capture the heart of God.

Prayer Focus:
I need to attract the presence of God.

- I have a need to draw His attention.
- I want to captivate His divine love.
- I want to be able to stand against the foe.
- I want to be able to declare my stand against the enemy.

The Authority of Scripture:
Deuteronomy 7:8; Jeremiah 31:3

The Prayer:
Lord I praise You. You are the King of Kings. Lord, I bless you. You are the Lord of lords. You are my rock and my fortress.

You are my strong tower.
In You I trust and rest my life.

Prayer of Confrontation:
Satan, listen to me.

Because of the Lord of Jesus Christ, you cannot touch.

Because of the Lord of Jesus Christ, you cannot invade my life.

Therefore, I command you to vacate from my home right now.

I command you to pack your luggages and depart from my residence.

In the name of Jesus Christ, I command to go and never to return.

In the name of Jesus Christ, you will no longer be my host.

Jesus Christ is my Lord and my Savior.

He died to set me free; therefore, I now belong to Jesus Christ. Amen!

Observations – write your experience after the prayer:

_____
_____
_____

Achievements – what did you gain from this prayer?

_____
_____
_____

CHAPTER TWENTY-EIGHT

Warring With Worship

Confront the enemy with praise and worship. The enemy will flee seven ways. The devil does not like it when God is being praise and worshipped.

The Word: Approach God with worship and adoration. Tell God who he is to you: 2 Samuel 22:2-3

> **The LORD is my rock and my fortress and my deliverer;**
> **My God, my strength, In whom I trust;**
> **My shield and the horn of my salvation, my stronghold.**
> **I will call upon the LORD,**
> **who is worthy to be praised;**
> **So shall I be saved from my enemies.**

Prayer Tactics
(Remember to observe the Spiritual Protocol)

State the Problem:
To be able to confront the enemy with praise and worship.

Prayer Focus:
Teach me to worship you in spirit and in truth

The Authority of Scripture:
Deuteronomy 32:4; 2 Samuel 22:2-3

The Prayer:
The Prayer:
Yes, Lord, You are my rock and my salvation.
Your name is power and authority.
There is healing in Your name.
There is deliverance in Your name.
The power of deliverance is in You.

Therefore, I am depending on You to deliver me from all evils as I stand in Your presence to ask for power to subdue the enemy.

Empower me to fight against the enemy and to overcome him in the name of Jesus. Amen!

Observations – write your experience after the prayer:

_____
_____
_____

Achievements – what did you gain from this prayer?

_____
_____
_____

CHAPTER TWENTY-NINE

Confronting With Scripture

—⚊—

The Word *(Scriptural Confrontation):* make your request known and say what the problem is. The pang of death is a sudden disaster or an accident that comes your way:

Psalm 18:4-5:

**The pangs of death surrounded me,
And the floods of ungodliness made me afraid.
The sorrows of Sheol surrounded me;
The snares of death confront me.**

Prayer Tactics
(Remember to observe the <u>Spiritual Protocol</u>)

State the Problem:
    Confronting the pangs of death.

Prayer Focus:
Need to break any link with the spirit of death.

The Authority of Scripture: Matthew 6:13

The Prayer of Confrontation:
The pangs of death shall no longer surround me, and the floods of ungodliness shall no longer threaten me.

I command the spirit of fear and disaster to go out of my life right now in the name of Jesus.

Whatever causes accident and disaster will not interfere with me.

The spirit of fear of the devil will not terrorize my life, and because of the blood of Jesus, it will no longer surround me

You pangs of death, go out of my life in the name of Jesus.

Go out of my mind, out of my body, out of my soul and out of my spirit in the name of Jesus.

In the name of Jesus, you no longer have authority over my life in the name of Jesus. I ask the blood of Jesus to surround me and to build a wall of protection over my life in Jesus' name. Amen!

Oh you sorrows of Sheol (hell), I command you to go out of my life.

You will no longer surround me, for the blood of Jesus is my protection.

Oh, you snare of death,

In the name of Jesus, I command you to leave me alone; you will no longer confront me.

The blood of Jesus sets me free from all manner of sorrows and snares.

Because of Jesus Christ my Lord and Savior, you shall no longer confront me.

For the Lord is my refuge, and He has delivered me from your sorrows and snares in Jesus' name. Amen.

Observations – write your experience after the prayer:

_____
_____
_____

Achievements – what did you gain from this prayer?

_____
_____
_____

CHAPTER THIRTY

On the Battlefield

—⚋—

The Word *(at the battlefront):* Express God's intervention at the battlefront as the war rages with fierce anger. As you fight, remember to fight in the name of the Lord and with the blood of Jesus. Remember to declare that God is your stronghold and your deliverer. God will certainly show up to defend you. He will never leave you alone in the front of the battle. He will send his angels to rescue you:

Psalm 18:6-7:

> **In my distress I called upon the LORD,**
> **And cried out to my God;**
> **he heard my voice from His temple,**
> **And my cry came before Him, even to His ears.**
>
> **Then the earth shook and trembled;**
> **The foundation of the hills also quaked**
> **and were shaken,**
> **Because he was angry.**

Prayer Tactics
(Remember to observe the <u>Spiritual Protocol</u>)

State the Problem:
Need boldness to stand against the wiles of the enemy.

Prayer Focus:
Need to declare boldness against fear of the devil.

The Authority of Scripture: Jeremiah 33:3

The Prayer of Confrontation:
Listen Satan, the Lord is my refuge and fortress.
Therefore, I command you to tremble in the name of Jesus.
With the authority in the blood of Jesus,
Satan I command your strongholds to be scattered right now in the name of Jesus.
I release confusion into the midst of your strongmen in the name of Jesus
The blood of Jesus overcomes you.
In the name of Jesus, you shall no longer plunder me. Amen!

Observations – write your experience after the prayer:

_____
_____
_____

Achievements – what did you gain from this prayer?

_____
_____
_____

CHAPTER THIRTY-ONE

The Joshua Strategy

The Word: The Joshua strategy gives us an idea of what happened between Israel and Ai when God motivated Joshua to fight against Ai. God Himself was at the war front as the commanding general with Joshua (Joshua 8:18-29).

Joshua's strategy also gives us the idea that prayer of warfare and confrontations involve military tactic; such as walking and marching around, pacing up and down, jumping and galloping, and also throwing hands around as in boxing and wrestling. Physical aggression is part of the military actions that are usually observed during active prayer of warfare and confrontations.

Psalm 18:8-12:

> **Smoke went up from His nostrils,**
> **And devouring fire from His mouth;**
> **Coals were kindled by it.**

**He bowed the heavens also, and came down
With darkness under His feet.
And He rode upon a cherub, and flew;
He flew upon the wings of the wind.
He made darkness His secret place;
His canopy around Him was dark waters
And thick clouds of the skies.
From the brightness before Him,
His thick clouds passed with hailstones
and coals of fire.**

Prayer Tactics
(Remember to observe the <u>Spiritual Protocol</u>)

State the Problem:

Need wisdom to plan strategies against the enemy.

Prayer Focus:

Need divine intervention to fight my wars.

The Authority of Scripture: Joshua 8:18-29

The War:

Satan, I declare you a loser in the name of Jesus Christ.

For every knee shall bow and every tongue confess that Jesus Christ is Lord.

The battle is the Lord's, and

He has conquered in the name of Jesus.

Observations – write your experience after the prayer:

_____
_____
_____

Achievements – what did you gain from this prayer?

_____
_____
_____

CHAPTER THIRTY-TWO

Jehovah's Strategy

The Word: Expression of Jehovah God's approach to war. God is great and mighty. His anger shakes the foundation of the earth and causes thunder and lightening to strike the enemy. The words of our mouths cannot describe the mighty hand of God in battle. Indeed He is the mighty warrior great in battle:

Psalm 18:13-15:

> **The LORD thundered from heaven,**
> **And the Most High uttered His voice,**
> **Hailstones and coals of fire.**
> **He sent out His arrows and scattered the foe,**
> **Lightnings in abundance, and He vanquished them.**
> **Then the channels of the sea were seen,**
> **The foundations of the world were uncovered**
> **At Your rebuke, O LORD,**
> **At the blast of the breath of Your nostrils.**

Prayer Tactics
(Remember to observe the Spiritual Protocol)

State the Problem:
That the Lord will take over my battles

Prayer Focus:
That I will surrender my battles to the Lord

- That I will allow God to be great in my challenges

The Authority of Scripture: Joshua 8:18-29

The War:
In the name of Jesus,

I command hailstones and fire to rain down upon the strongholds of my enemies.

Yes, Lord, release the hailstones and fire against the stronghold of my enemies,

That they may know that You are the God of yesterday, today and forever.

Like the days of Sodom and Gomorrah, in the name of Jesus, turn the days of my enemies into darkness, and strike them with blindness that they may not see me and touch me.

Observations – write your experience after the prayer:

_____
_____
_____

Achievements – what did you gain from this prayer?

_____
_____
_____

CHAPTER THIRTY-THREE

Divine Deliverance

The Word: Describe the experience of God's deliverance in a fierce war. There is no god like Jehovah God. Indeed He has proved Himself the Man of War. The Ancient of Days, and we must acknowledge His mighty prowess.

Psalm 18:16-19:

> He sent from above, He took me;
> He drew me out of many waters.
> He delivered me from my strong enemy,
> From those who hated me,
> For they were too strong for me.
> They confronted me in the day of my calamity,
> But the LORD was my support.
> He also brought me out into a broad place;
> He delivered me because he delighted in me.

Prayer Tactics
(Remember to observe the <u>Spiritual Protocol</u>)

State the Problem:
To acknowledge the greatness of God in my life

Prayer Focus:
To understand divine protection

The Authority of Scripture: Psalm 23

The Deliverance Prayer:
Satan, I raise a standard against you in the name of Jesus.
The Most High God is greater than you.
Yeah though I walk in the valley of the shadow of death,
I will fear no evil, for the Lord is with me.
Therefore, Satan, you are a defeated foe.
Because of Jesus Christ my Lord and Savior, you shall not stand before me.
Amen!

Observations – write your experience after the prayer:

_____
_____
_____

Achievements – what did you gain from this prayer?

_____
_____
_____

CHAPTER THIRTY-FOUR

The Victory

The Word: Declare your victory in the name of Jesus. Exalt the name of the Lord and praise Him. Lift high the banner of victory.

Psalm 18:20-50:

> The LORD rewarded me according to my righteousness;
> According to the cleanness of my hands
> He has recompensed me
> For I have kept the ways of the LORD,
> And have not wickedly departed from my God.
> For all His judgments were before me,
> And I did not put away His statutes from me.
> I was also blameless before Him,
> And I kept myself from my iniquity.
> Therefore, the LORD has recompensed me according to my righteousness,

According to the cleanness of my hands in His sight.

The Deliverance:

The Word:

With the merciful You will show Yourself merciful;
With a blameless man
You will show Yourself blameless;
With the pure You will show Yourself pure;
And with the devious You will show Yourself shrewd.
For You will save the humble people,
But will bring down haughty looks.
For You will light my lamp;
The LORD my God will enlighten my darkness.
For by You I can run against a troop,
By my God I can leap over a wall.
As for God, His way is perfect;
The word of the LORD is proven;
He is a shield to all who trust Him.

The Victory: Sing the song of victory.

For who is God, except the LORD?
And who is a rock except our God?
It is God who arms me with strength,
and makes my way perfect.
He makes my feet like the feet of a deer,

And sets me on high places.
34. He teaches my arms to make war,
so that my hands can bend a bow of bronze.

The Celebration: Celebrate the Name of Jesus as your deliverer.

You have also given me the shield of You salvation;
Your right hand has help me up,
Your gentleness has made me great.
You enlarged my path under me,
So my feet did not slip.
I have pursued my enemies and overtaken them;
Neither did I turn back again till they were destroyed.
I have wounded them,
So that they could not rise;
They have fallen under my feet.
For You have armed me with the strength for battle;
You have subdued under me, those who rose up against me.
You have also given me the neck of my enemies,
So that I destroyed those who hated me.
They cried out, but there was none to save;
Even to the LORD, but he did not answer them.
Then I beat them as fine as the dust before the wind;

I cast them out like dirt in the streets.
You have delivered me from the strivings of the people;
You have made me the head of nations;
A people I have not known shall serve me.
As soon as they hear of me they obey me;
The foreigners submit to me.
The foreigners fade away,
And come frightened from their hideouts.
The LORD lives!
Blessed be my Rock!
Let the God of my salvation be exalted.
It is God who avenges me,
And subdues the peoples under me;
He delivers me from my enemies.
You also lift me up above those who rise against me;
You have delivered me from the violet man.
Therefore, I will give thanks to You, O LORD, among the Gentiles,
And sing praises to Your name.
50. Great deliverance He brings to His king,
And shows mercy to His anointed,
To David and his descendants forevermore.

Prayer Tactics
(Remember to observe the Spiritual Protocol)

State the Problem:
That I may acknowledge and celebrate the Lord Jesus Christ as my Overcomer.

Prayer Focus:
I need to understand the victory that I have in Christ Jesus.

- I need to celebrate Him as my Overcomer.
- I need to accept Him as my Victor.
- I need to hail him as my Conqueror.

The Authority of Scripture: 1 Samuel 17:37

The Prayer:
Lord, I lift up Your name as my Savior
who saves me from all manner of evil.
I praise Your name as my as my Redeemer
who redeems me by His blood.
Lord, I honor You as my Conqueror
who fights all battles on my behalf.
I worship You as my Victor
who wins all battles for me
Your name is worthy to be praised.
Your name is victory and I shall praise You forever. Amen!

Observations – write your experience after the prayer:

_____
_____
_____

Achievements – what did you gain from this prayer?

_____
_____
_____

CHAPTER THIRTY-FIVE

Praying with John 1

In the beginning was the Word, and the Word was with God, and the Word was God.

He was in the beginning with God.

All things were made through Him, and without Him nothing was made that was made.

Prayer:

Listen, Satan, I am created by the Word of God from the very beginning, and the Word of God is in me. Therefore, I speak the Word of God with power and authority in the name of Jesus Christ, and I declare the Word of God over my life in Jesus' name.

In Him was life, and the life was the light of men.

And the light shines in the darkness, and the darkness did not comprehend it.

Prayer Tactics
(Remember to observe the Spiritual Protocol)

State the Problem:
That I may understand the power of the spoken Word of God.

Prayer Focus:
That the word of will make impact in me as I read and speak it into my life.

The Authority of Scripture: John 1:1-5

The Prayer:
Lord, I praise You as the Alpha and Omega because You are the beginning of all beginnings.
Scripture declares that You were in the beginning and Your Word has always been with You.
Lord, I lift up Your name because Your Word is life, and it is the light that shines in darkness.
When light comes darkness must depart.
Therefore, I receive the Word of God and I declare into my life right now, in the name of Jesus Christ, I command darkness to disappear as I command the Word of God to shine all over me right now.
In the beginning was the Word and the Word was with God,
Therefore, I leave the Word of God to engulf my whole life.
In the name of Jesus, I saturate my life with the Word that Your presence might shine around me. Amen!

Observations – write your experience after the prayer:

_____
_____
_____

Achievements – what did you gain from this prayer?

_____
_____
_____

CHAPTER THIRTY-SIX

Praying with Psalm 91

Psalm 91 is the Scripture weapon for warring against witches and other workers of iniquity.

> **HE who dwells in the secret place of the Most High**
> **Shall abide under the shadow of the Almighty.**
> **will say of the LORD, "He is my refuge and my fortress;**
> **My God, in Him I will trust."**

Prayer:
The Lord has become my refuge since I accepted Jesus Christ as my Lord and Savior. The Lord has become my hiding place and my fortress. My trust in Him is sure and I cannot be touched by the enemy.

**Surely He shall deliver you from the snare of the fowler
And from the perilous pestilence.
He shall cover you with His feathers,
And under His wings you shall take refuge;
His truth shall be your truth and buckler.
You shall not be afraid of the terror by night,
Nor of the arrows that fly by day,
Nor of the pestilence that walks in darkness,
Nor of the destruction that lays waste at noonday.**

Prayer:

Hey, Satan, I shall no longer be afraid of you, and you shall no longer threaten me, because I am no longer under your control. The Lord has delivered me from your perilous pestilence and I declare my freedom in Jesus name. The blood of Jesus Christ repels your terrors and nullifies your arrows. In the name of Jesus Christ, your terror and arrow can no longer interfere with me. Because of the blood of Jesus Christ, the spirit of darkness can no longer visit me. Light has come, therefore, darkness is defeated in the name of Jesus.

**A thousand may fall at your side,
And ten thousand at *your* right hand;
But it shall not come near you.
Only with your eyes shall you look,
And see the reward of the wicked.**

Strategic Prayer Tactics II

Prayer:
Hey, Satan, tens of your thousands cannot stand the blood and the cross of Jesus Christ. Jesus has siezed the keys of death. The grave could not hold Him captive; therefore, you cannot hold me captive.

> **Because you have made the LORD, who is my refuge,**
> **Even the Most High, your dwelling place,**
> **No evil shall befall you,**
> **Nor shall any plague come near your dwelling;**
> **For He shall give His angels charge over you.**
> **To keep you in all your ways.**
> **In their hands they shall bear you up,**
> **Lest you dash your foot against a stone.**
> **You shall tread upon the lion and the cobra,**
> **The young lion and the serpent you shall trample underfoot.**

Prayer:
The Lord has promised to be my refuge so long as I dwell in Him.

The Lord has promised that no evil shall befall me, nor would any plague come near me, for He shall give His angels charge over me. I stand on the promises of the Lord, and I declare Him as my habitation in the name of Jesus Christ. Yeah, though I walk through the valley of the shadow of death, I shall fear no evil. Yeah though I tread upon the lion and the cobra, I shall not be hurt, because the Lord is my refuge and my fortress. I thank you, Lord, for being my refuge and my fortress against the wiles of the devil.

> Because he has set his love upon Me, therefore I will deliver him;
> I will set him on high; because he has known My name.
> He shall call upon Me, and I will answer him;
> I will be with him in trouble;
> I will deliver him and honor him.
> With long life I will satisfy him,
> And show him My salvation."

Prayer:

Lord, I thank You for Your promise of protection and deliverance.

I thank You for giving me Your name above all other names.

I thank You for giving me the privilege to call upon You and that You will answer.

I give You the praise and adoration for blessing me with long life and salvation.

I thank You, Lord, for such a wonderful expression of love over my life. Amen!

Observations – write your experience after the prayer:

_____
_____
_____

Achievements – what did you gain from this prayer?

_____
_____
_____

DECISION

If you have never surrendered your life to Jesus Christ as your Lord and Savior, then it would be better for you to do so right away. Otherwise, it will be difficult for you to rule over anger and the bunch of negatives ruling your life. If you are willing to accept Jesus Christ as your Lord and Savior, then pray like this:

Lord Jesus, I come to you just as I am. Forgive me my sins and deliver me from all works of iniquity.

Deliver me from all the evil characters and behaviors that have kept me in bondage.

Set my soul and spirit free to worship you in spirit and in truth.

Come into my life and make me whole.

I need you, Lord. I need you every hour unto eternity. Amen.

REDEDICATION

If you have ever made a decision to surrender your life to Jesus Christ, and you have been struggling with the Christian life, or you are somehow an active Christian but still struggling with some ungodly characters and behaviors, then you need to rededicate yourself to the Lordship of your Jesus. Make a total surrender, so that the enemy will not have any form of control at all in your life. You may pray like this:

Lord Jesus, teach me to surrender my total being to your Lordship and control, that the enemy will no longer have a part in me. Teach me to abide in you so that you would also abide in me and dwell in my life.

Teach me to study your Word and make conscious effort to apply such to my daily living.

Wash me, cleanse me, and purify my spirit, soul and body that I may be acceptable in your sight.

Thank you, Lord, for delivering me from the works of iniquity. Amen.

Pauline Walley School of Intensive Training For Ministry and Leadership Equipment (PW-SITME)

The Pauline Walley School of Intensive Training for Ministry Equipment is an institution for training leaders, individuals and church groups. It is an intensive practical training center where people are taught to build their image and personality, improve their ministry skills and abilities, develop their talents and gifts, minister to self, family members, friends and to church or fellowship members. In the process of training, people are also taught to be equipped for ministration and to face the battle of life as it is in the ministry.

The areas of study are:

School of Deliverance (SOD)
School of Strategic Prayer (SSP)
School of Tactical Evangelism (STE)

School of Mentoring and Leadership (SML)
School of the Gifts of the Holy Spirit (SGHS)
School of the Prophets (SOP)

The Pauline Walley School of Intensive Training programs are organized and held in different parts of the world at various times. At seminar levels, one week or two weeks of intensive training are organized to help leaders and ministers or church/fellowship groups to establish various arms of Church ministry and also equip their members for such purposes.

Bi-weekly intensive training programs and one-year certificate course is readily available in Bronx, New York and other regions based on request. If you are interested in hosting any of these programs in your region or country or church/ministry, please contact us. *See details of our contact and website on the back page.*

About the School of Deliverance

The School of Deliverance is an institution for training leaders, individuals and church groups on how to minister deliverance. It is a practical training course where people are taught to minister to self, family members, friends and to church or fellowship members. In the process of training, people are also taught to be equipped for ministration and to face the battle of life as it is in the ministry.

The areas of study are in four modules. The first module focuses on "how to minister deliverance;" the second on "how to pull down satanic strongholds;" the third module is on "how to maintain your deliverance;" and the fourth module is on the "techniques of ministrations."

The School of Deliverance is organized and held in different parts of the world at various times. At seminar levels, one week or two weeks of intensive training are organized to help leaders and ministers or church/fellowship groups to establish a deliverance ministry or equip their members for such purposes.

Intensive training and a one-year certificate course is readily available in Bronx, New York and other regions based on request. If you are interested in hosting the School of Deliverance in your region or country or church/ministry, please contact us. *See details of our contact and website on the back page.*

Christian Books
By
DR. PAULINE WALLEY

THE AUTHORITY OF AN OVERCOMER:
YOU CAN HAVE IT . . . I HAVE IT
The Authority of an Overcomer shares the real-life testimony of a day-to-day experience with the Lord Jesus Christ. It encourages you to apply the Word of God to every facet of your life, such as sleeping and waking with Jesus, walking and talking with Jesus, and dining with Him as you would with your spouse or a friend.

SOMEBODY CARES . . . CARES FOR YOU . . .
CARES FOR ME
Somebody Cares . . . Cares for you . . . Cares for Me talks about the care that the Lord Almighty has for every one of us. It teaches you to care for other people and exercise tolerance towards their short-

comings. You will learn the importance of love and the true meaning as you read this book

RECEIVE AND MAINTAIN YOUR DELIVERANCE ON LEGAL GROUNDS.

Many people go from one prayer house to another, from the general practitioner to the specialist, from one minister to the pope; and from one chapel to another church, with the same mission, aiming for the same expectation, yet, never hitting the target. Why? Many people lack the knowledge of maintaining their healing and deliverance. This book: *Receive and Maintain Your Deliverance on Legal Grounds* will teach you to understand how to maintain what you receive from God.

ANGER: GET RID OF IT . . . YOU CAN OVERCOME IT

Anger is one of the many problems that many seek to resolve but lack the solution. Many have resigned their fate to it, thinking that it is a natural phenomenon. This book teaches about the causes of anger, and how to uproot them to receive your healing.

THE POWER OF THE SPOKEN WORD

There is a purpose for which we speak, and when we speak, we expect something to happen in order for the purpose of the utterance to be fulfilled. This book teaches you to exercise your authority so that the word that you speak will be manifested effectively.

THE HOLY SPIRIT: THE UNIQUENESS OF HIS PRESENCE.

The presence of the Holy Spirit highlights the difference between the gifts of the Spirit, the presence of God and the visitation of the Holy Spirit. In this book you will learn to enjoy the delightful presence of the Holy Spirit in your spiritual walk.

THE HOLY SPIRIT: MAINTAIN HIS PRESENCE IN TRIALS AND TEMPTATIONS

This book teaches you how to maintain the presence of God, especially in trials and temptations. Oftentimes, when Christians go through difficult situations, they think they are alone. But that need not be. You can enter the presence of the Holy Spirit in difficult times and witness His Power to strengthen you and turn your situations around.

THE HOLY SPIRIT: POWER OF THE TONGUE

In recent times, many people have been seeking instant power and prophetic manifestations. Christians and ministers are indulging in all sorts of practices to demonstrate some special abilities to attract public attention. This book, *Power of the Tongue*, discusses the various powers and anointing(s) at work. It will help you to decipher between the Holy Spirit power and satanic powers. It will also teach you about the various anointing(s) that exist and how you can reach out for the genuine one.

PULLING DOWN SATANIC STRONGHOLDS: WAR AGAINST EVIL SPIRITS

Many Christians are under satanic attacks and influences, but very few people understand what the actual problems are. Some believe in God, but have no idea that there is anything like the satanic realm, yet they are under satanic torments. This book, Pulling Down Satanic Strongholds, enlightens you on some of the operations of the devil. It will help you know when an activity being performed around you is of the devil. This knowledge will strengthen you in prayer and equip you against the wiles of the enemy.

WHEN SATAN WENT TO CHURCH?

Many people fear the devil more than they fear God. At the mention of Satan or demons, they are threatened to death. Yet they are complacent in their own ways and yield to sin easily. Let the fear of God grip you and not the fear of Satan. This book enlightens you on the activities of the enemy within and around the church, the home and the Christian community. It helps you to identify battles and to put on your armor of warfare against the enemy. It also encourages you to hold firm the shield of faith. May the Lord enlighten your eyes of understanding as you read this book.

SOLUTION: DELIVERANCE MINISTRATION TO SELF AND OTHERS

Since the death of Jesus Christ on the cross, humans have been given the opportunity to experience and encounter the joy of salvation. However, lack of knowledge has kept the world in the dark and deprived them of the importance of Christianity. This book, *Solution: Deliverance Ministration to Self and Others* portrays just what the title says. It teaches you to understand the intricacies of deliverance ministration and to avoid the dangerous practices that have discouraged others. Read it and you will be blessed as never before.

STRATEGIC PRAYER TACTICS I: EFFECTIVE COMMUNICATIONS WITH AROMATIC EXPRESSIONS

This book, *Strategic Prayer Tactics I*, with focus on types and approaches to prayer teaches you how to approach the throne of God with a specific need and the strategies to adopt for presentation. It also teaches you to pray with Scripture as your legal authority. Read it and you will be blessed as never before.

STRATEGIC PRAYER TACTICS II: EFFECTIVE DELIVERANCE PRAYER TACTICS; WARFARE AND CONFRONTATIONS APPROACH TO EFFECTIVE COMMUNICATION IN PRAYER

This book, Effective Deliverance Prayer Tactics teaches you how to approach the throne of God with a specific need and the strategies to adopt for presentation. It also teaches you to pray with Scripture as your legal authority. Read it and you will be blessed as never before.

SCHOOL OF MENTORING AND LEADERSHIP I:
THE ACT OF MENTORING
STIRRING UP, ACTIVATING AND IMPARTING TALENTS AND ABILITIES FOR EFFECTIVENESS

Everyone has talents and abilities that need to be developed in order for a person to achieve an ambition. Many people are bedeviled by unfulfilled dreams and are wallowing in familiar oppression and depression. This book will help you to locate and choose a mentor, who will help you to discover and develop your abilities that will lead you into fulfilling your ambition. This course will teach and draw you closer to your destiny. Stay blessed and enjoy the Act of Mentoring.

SCHOOL OF MENTORING AND LEADERSHIP II: PROGRESSIVE ACHIEVEMENT – RECEIVE IT; MAINTAIN IT.
THE ACT OF SELF-MENTORING

This book, *Progressive Achievement: Receive it; Maintain It*, teaches you how to mentor yourself while you move in progression to overcome obstacles that would usually frustrate prosperity. It enlightens you about the various types of progress that may come your way and how to manage them. It also encourages you to overcome failure and disappointment. The book also helps you to understand the concept of self-mentoring in the course of progressiveness as part of the characteristics of the Holy Spirit.

Subscription

—∿—

GOSPEL SONGS ON CASSETTE
Overcomers' Expression
Send Your Power
Vessels of Worship
Poetic Expression

BOOKS
All the books listed can be ordered

CONTACT: For Ministration

WEST AFRICA
Pauline Walley School of Deliverance
P.O. Box MS 301, Mile-Seven, Accra, Ghana.
Tel/Fax: (233) 403063 or 404184

UNITED KINGDOM
Pauline Walley Christian Communications
P.O. Box 4673, London SE1 4UQ.
Tel: (44) 794-769-7867

UNITED STATES
Pauline Walley Christian Communications
P. O. Box 250, Bronx, NY 10467
Telephone (718) 652-2916/Fax (718) 405-2035
Email: paulinewalley@optonline.net
(or) pauline@paulinewalley.org
Website: www.school-of-deliverance.com
www.paulinewalley.org

CPSIA information can be obtained at www.ICGtesting.com
Printed in the USA
LVOW060937041212

309973LV00001B/48/A